# A SYMPOSIUM ON ETHICS

## The Role of Moral Values in Contemporary Thought

Edited by

### Bernard Den Ouden
University of Hartford

UNIVERSITY
PRESS OF
AMERICA

Copyright © 1982 by

**University Press of America, Inc.**

P.O. Box 19101, Washington, D.C. 20036

All rights reserved

Printed in the United States of America

ISBN (Perfect): 0-8191-2764-7
ISBN (Cloth): 0-8191-2763-9

DEDICATION

The following essays are dedicated to the students and faculty of the University of Hartford.

## ACKNOWLEDGEMENTS

Many individuals contributed to the development of the symposium and of this volume. I am especially indebted to Mahlon Barnes, Carol Dalphin, Marcia Moen and May Nevius for their careful assistance in proofreading. If there are errors that remain I am responsible for them. Carol Guardo's support in spirit and funding was essential to the planning and execution of this project. She is deserving of special thanks.

## TABLE OF CONTENTS

INTRODUCTION   Bernard Den Ouden                ix

PAPER I   VALUES AND COMMUNITY   Mahlon W. Barnes   1

    Comment:   Stephen White
                 Richard Lee

PAPER II   ETHICS IN JOURNALISM   Theodore L. Glasser   17

    Comment:   George Michael Evica
                 Stephen Norland

PAPER III   LIFE AND ART   Jonathan Bushnell Bakker   43

    Comment:   Christopher Horton
                 Sherry Buckberrough

PAPER IV   WAR AND MORALITY   Peter K. Breit   69

    Comment:   Julian W. Streitfeld
                 James Etzweiler

INTRODUCTION

On April 28, 1981, a Symposium on Ethics was held at the University of Hartford. The topic for discussion was the "Role of Moral Values in Contemporary Thought". The University's Philosophy Department invited contributions from all academic disciplines and selected four that most directly examined the theme of the Symposium. This was done out of recognition that many disciplines who had championed "value for inquiry" were returning to an examination of ethical issues.

The papers that comprise this volume are those presented at this conference and have been revised for publication. They are scholars speaking with scholars in a manner that the interested public will find accessible. In a time when moral issues are discussed in a volatile and frequently politically manipulative fashion, it is particularly important to have experts examine these issues with the resources of their respective disciplines. This volume is one such attempt.

The first paper at the conference was presented by Mahlon Barnes of the Department of Philosophy of the University of Hartford. Responding to his works were Richard Lee of Trinity College and Stephen White formerly of the Department of Politics and Government of the University of Hartford and presently a member of the Department of Political Science of Virginia Polytechnical Institute. The second paper was presented by Theodore L. Glasser formerly of the Department of Communications of the University of Hartford. Professor Glasser presently holds a visiting appointment at the School of Journalism and Mass Communications of the University of Minnesota. Responding to his presentation were George Michael Evica of the University of Hartford's English Department and Stephen Norland, Director of the Criminal Justice program at the University.

The third paper was presented by Jonathan Bushnell Bakker formerly of the University of Hartford's Philosophy Department and presently teaching at the University of Rhode Island. Respondents to Jonathan's works were Sherry Buckberrough who chairs the Department of Art History of the University of Hartford and Christopher Horton who is an Associate Professor of the Hartford Art School.

The final paper was presented by Peter K. Breit, Chairman of the Department of Politics and Government of the University of Hartford. Respondents to his paper were Julian Streitfeld, Professor of Psychology at the University and James Etzweiler, Chairman of the Department of Philosophy of St. Joseph's College. Carol Guardo, Provost of the University of Hartford provided funding for the conference through her office and gave the opening remarks. Bernard Den Ouden, Chairman of the Department of Philosophy moderated the discussion. The presentations were broadcast on Connecticut Public Radio during July and August in the summer of 1981.

A limited number of copies of this anthology are available from the Department of Philosophy of the University of Hartford upon request.

PAPER I

VALUES AND COMMUNITY

M.W. Barnes

It is no longer as widely believed as it once was that values, or "value judgements," must be entirely excluded from serious thought. It has never been claimed, of course, that the existence of value judgements should be ignored altogether. They should be noted where relevant, treated as historical or biographical facts that need explanation. However, it was thought that the inquirer must not treat values as having any validity, and above all, the inquirer must not make any judgements. Thus, for example, the anthropologist may note the acceptance somewhere of ritual murder, but may not ask whether it is right or say that it is wrong. The critic may note that a poet celebrates certain values, but is barred from asking whether those values are perverse or destructive. This attitude often went so far as to lead to the claim that explanations of one's actions in terms of value are always rationalizations, masking motives to which the value statements are irrelevant.

There are a number of reasons for holding this view. One of them is the justified desire to avoid the mistake of supposing that what we think ought to be the case really is the case. As an example, there is the widespread medieval belief that the orbits of the planets must satisfy some aesthetic requirements. Closely allied to this reason for value neutrality on the part of the inquirer is the recognition that the inquirer's values may prejudice and distort observation, for example causing an anthropologist to see non-literate societies as nothing but immoral savages. Still another reason, certainly, is the plausible but mistaken belief that value neutrality guarantees tolerance and avoids conflict.

While all these considerations were important, there was one reason that was still more influential in producing the insistence on value neutrality, namely the belief that values lack objectivity. Objectivity is a confused and confusing notion, but the problem is not difficult to see. If I believe that the world is round, I can, at least in principle, point to evidence for that belief, evidence that is available to others and that supports its probability. Even if the belief is a false one, an appeal to evidence can be made, in that case unsuccessfully. But if I claim that murder is wrong, it is difficult to see that there could be evidence for that. There is evidence that murder is undesirable, of course, namely that allowing murder has consequences that most of us do not want, but that seems not to be the same thing. You cannot relevantly respond to a claim that murder is wrong by saying, "Yes, I know that most people don't want the consequences of murder, but I do." Saying that murder is wrong means that you ought not to commit murder, whether you accept the consequences or not. And while moral values provide the most obvious instances, the same sort of thing can be said for other values. Try offering evidence that Hamlet is a great drama.

The same cannot be said, however, for valuations, if that word is understood as meaning actual preferences or aversions in particular situations. That a person, or for that matter any animal, has a preference for something, that it is valued in that sense, is always in principle capable of being evidenced. It is not surprising, therefore, that values were admitted into inquiry only if they could be treated as valuations.

This attitude has changed in recent years. When John Gardner published On Moral Fiction he was criticized for taking a rather dogmatic tone and for naming names, but there was little resistance to his suggestion that literature has a moral purpose and can be criticized in terms of that purpose. Twenty years ago he would have had difficulty finding a publisher. A new, younger generation of social scientists, I am told, has come into being who claim that the value neutrality of their elders is irresponsible, and hint that they persist in it out of servility or moral cowardice. Nobody, of course, wants to go back to the bad old days when critics let the moral tendency of a poem make up for poor craftsmanship or lost sight of real poetic merit in a fit of moral indignation. Nobody with any intellectual integrity wants social scientists to become propagandists or biological conclusions tailored to a supposed need for moral uplift.

Value has to come back: but how? The actual incorporation of value into the humanities and sciences will have to be left to the specialists in those fields--after all, there are limits to a philosopher's helpfulness. What I want to do is sketch a general theory of the nature of value that may be of use for those who must find a way of restoring value to intellectual respectability. There are some general requirements such a theory will have to meet, in order to be true to our experience and our intuitions.

First, since it is an assumption that has clearly failed in the past, we will expect that our account of value will not permit the inference that what is must somehow conform to what ought to be. This eliminates the naive notions of Divine Providence that dominated so much medieval science; that is, even if we accept the idea that our sense of value is an awareness of a system of values somehow inherent in the universe, that system does not so dominate reality as to allow the inference from what is good to what is true.

Second, our conception of the nature of value must do full justice to the fallibility of our value judgements. This is a rather complex matter, but it begins easily enough. Interpretation of art, of other cultures, and of the past has often been nothing but moral censure. I have already noted that the demand for value neutrality was partly a reaction against that tendency. The people who indulged in that moral censure could hardly have done so if they were not unjustifiably certain as to what the "true" values were. Now anyone who makes such a claim to certainty is mistaken. After all, even if you had a signed message from God, you could not be sure you had read it correctly; and given the complexity of human life, the message would have to be so long that nobody could read it all. Most of it would be fine print, explaining how to apply general principles to particular cases.

We cannot be certain of our values. That is the easy part. The hard part is that we still have to act, and are thus not allowed the luxury of skepticism. We cannot act as though we doubted our own values, and we cannot avoid moral criticism of others on a skeptical basis. In short, while we must take account of our fallibility with regard to values, we must not do so in a way that would paralyze action and prevent dialogue. The reference to criticism may come as a surprise to some; but to refuse to enter into value dialogue with others is to fail to take them seriously, to act as though their actions do not matter. The detail is difficult to work out, but the general principle is clear: value must not be conceived in such a way that our lack of certainty prevents our acting or gives us an excuse for ignoring value altogether.

This last really means that value must have a function in human life. Our conception of value must be such as to take account of the functions it does have. The main function seems to be in criticism, where criticism is to be understood not as censure but as dialogue with the aim of mutual improvement. As a model we might take the good literary critic who discusses a writer's work in a way that can aid in improving it, while not fearing to reveal inadequacies in the critic's own apprehension that, when corrected, can lead to a greater sensitivity. Not only do artist and critic gain from such an interchange, but if it is carried on in public, the bystanders also gain. Criticism thus refers both to the past and the future, as evaluation of the past out of concern for the future. Understanding criticism in this sense, we can say that values must be capable of functioning in mutual criticism and self-criticism. A little later I will suggest that there can be no sharp distinction between individual and society, but it is still possible to say that values function in criticism of individuals by society and of society by individuals. This is not a trivial point; it is rather easy to fall into one of the equally absurd positions that individuals must always or must never accept the values of the society they live in.

It might be suggested that values have another function, as ideals: but what function is served by ideals? If we remember that one kind of criticism is self-criticism, we see that reference to ideals is merely one of the ways in which values are involved in criticism. If ideals are understood, as they all too often are, as unreachable states that we are all to be condemned for not reaching, we are better off without them. The function of an ideal is to regulate development, not to create grounds for guilt, hypocrisy, and despair.

Finally, values must be understood as facts in <u>concrete</u> human life. Even when our actions can be thought of as instances of a general type, they are never merely that. They happen at a particular time and place, in a definite context, with definite actions as their predecessors and successors. Most importantly, our actions happen in a real time, with a past that is no longer and a future that is not yet. We can write someone's biography, and it will seem as though all the events of that life are together, in the book, so that we could read them in whatever order we choose. But they were not lived that way. The subject of the biography made choices out of a remembered and interpreted past, in the expectation of a future that was never quite what he or she intended, and was nothing but an expectation until it happened. The only way we could write down a whole biography is in case the subject is dead.

Values cannot be merely individual, as valuations can. It is true that someone might hold a value that is idiosyncratic, that nobody else actually does hold, but to call it a value is to say that someone else might hold it, and further that anyone else must be able to recognize it as a possible regulating principle for action. It could not function in criticism, even self-criticism, if it were not so. Furthermore, values do not cause actions. If I say that I did something because I believe in (for example) human dignity, I am giving a reason, not a causal explanation, and reasons presuppose society. Even when our reasons are not actually involved in social dialogue, they are social in nature. Robinson Crusoe's values, like his words, presuppose society, even when he has nobody to talk to.

Society is not just an aggregate of individuals, which is why we cannot decide on values merely by vote. If there is consensus in some values, we may be justified in calling them "our values," or "the values of our society," but it is not the consensus that made them so. Rather, it is the fact that individuals found them useful in accounting for actions and in interpreting the actions of others. The fact that values guide individual action means that they cannot be entirely social, as does the fact that they can be appealed to by individuals in criticism of society. What makes the situation paradoxical is that values share in a peculiarity that haunts all meaningful human activity: the fact that we can express our individuality only by social means. All social action must be derived from individual action; but all individual action, insofar as it is meaningful enough to function in social action, must be interpretable in social terms.

Human life is interpreted life. We often talk about life having "meaning," but we have yet to take sufficiently seriously what that involves. Usually that expression is understood in terms of a life as a whole, or of human life in general, having a meaning, and most twentieth-century people have come to recognize that in that sense life either has no meaning or has a meaning that is radically unknowable. In another sense, however, all our actions have meanings. It is true that some of the events of our lives are occurrences that we think of as not really being our actions. Those actions that we do call ours are significant: they sum up a past and point to a future. They are what they are, for others, or even for ourselves, as a result of interpretation. To interpret an action is not merely to note its presence or to account for it as an instance of a general law. It is rather to see it as belonging to a system from which it derives its character. A person's actions belong primarily to two interconnected systems. One of them is that person's life, taken as a stream of events. In that stream each action derives meaning from its predecessors, as accounting for their direction; in doing so it transforms their meaning, for now they are comprehensible in terms of an outcome that was previously at most an intention. The present act is also future-directed, and will interpret and be interpreted in its turn by actions that are subsequent to it.

It is clear from this description that a stream of mutually interpreting actions is a dynamic system, requiring real, concrete time for its existence. Some people may be disturbed by the seeming suggestion that in such a system the past is changed. It is not, of course. The events of the past are permanently beyond the reach of any action. What changes is their significance. When Kant said of Plato that sometimes we understand a philosopher better than he understood himself, he was primarily thinking of the fact that Plato's thought is somehow changed by our knowledge of what later thinkers made of it. We have a Plato who was read by Kant; Plato did not. But that does not add a single letter to the <u>Republic</u>. This temporality is characteristic of interpretive systems, and abstractness, which robs them of their temporality, also robs them of their life.

The clearest recognition of the importance of seeing life as an interpretive system comes from our great, though practically unknown, American philosopher, Josiah Royce, who moreover, took the matter a step farther. Partly as a result of his early experiences in Gold Rush California--he was born there in 1855--Royce came to realize that even if it is conceived of as a dynamic system of mutually interpreting events, the notion of an individual human life is still an abstraction, because those systems are necessarily embedded in larger systems, the communities to which they belong. Containing as they do the relatively autonomous individual lives (characterized, Royce thought, by their individual projects that always function in their interpretation), the community cannot be thought of as a super-individual, but it shares with them the character of being a dynamic system of interpretations. Each life interprets itself, at least in part, by reference to its interpretation of and by the actions of others. To interpret another's actions is not to perform them, and I might understand what someone is doing without having the least inclination to do it. But they are a fact in my life, and I necessarily take account of them in my own acting. Further, the perspectives of the others, when interpreted in terms of my own life, provide me with a world that is not just mine, but a common world in which we can act. There is really little point in asking whether our communal dimension is or is not advantageous to us: it is an unavoidable, pervasive fact of our lives, and to the extent that we are deprived of it, our lives seem pointless.

Value is an aspect of that communal dimension. In community, a dimension emerges that is not present in individual life, namely the need to adjust action in view of interpretations not one's own. A little reflection shows us how much of our lives consists in interpreting the actions of others and making sure that they can interpret ours. It is not just the overt signalling, explicit interpretation, and verbal communication. We look at another person and know what he or she is doing. The interpretation is so automatic that we scarcely realize we are doing it. We also assume that others are doing the same for us, to the point that we are sometimes surprised when our actions are not understood. So important is this mutual interpretation to us, that in spite of our justified insistence on the right to privacy, we find it uncomfortable to refuse a request for explanation of our action.

When we are unable to use our repertory of automatic interpretations of actions, we must use dialogue. Most of it only incidentally involves values. Often we only seek information, asking to understand an action so that we may help or not hinder, and in any case so that we can properly act in response to the actions of others. Where value enters is with criticism. We should remember that criticism, as the word is used here, is not censure. Censure, like coercion, appears only when dialogue, and therefore community, fails. What criticism does involve is a proposal that some possible action is to be preferred to others, a proposal that may or may not be accepted. The values are involved as reasons for or against the preference.

At any stage in its history, a community will have a ready-made stock of reasons that can be offered. Arising as they do from collective experience, those reasons are far from being arbitrary, and since collective experience is less likely to be subject to the distortions of individual perspective, those "values of the society" have strong claims to validity. But they are fallible. The future will reinterpret them, and may do so in such a way as to amount to abandoning them. Individuals may find reasons to set them aside or apply them in new ways. Since they are never perfectly consistent with one another and their mutual relevance is always subject to doubt, dialogue about them is always possible, and in dialogue there is always the chance that novel values will be introduced.

If the values are not arbitrary, there must be reasons for them. They will be derived from the nature of community, and while most discussions of value will appeal to values already established, there are some underlying conditions that might be thought of as the foundations of value. They include:

1.  The furtherance of individual lives, of course in terms of continuation but more importantly in terms of significance.

2.  The furtherance of communal aims. Any community is partly defined by aims that are not those of specific individuals, but of individuals acting together.

3.  The maintenance of the dialogue that makes the community possible.

I do not know whether this list is complete. Certainly any community must have at least those interests, and it is perhaps worth pointing out that, while there is no guarantee that they could lead to a consistent and coherent system of values, the third condition, the maintenance of dialogue, demands that we act as though they could.

If this account is correct, value is neither individual nor social, but emerges out of the mutual interpretation of individuals in community. As such, value is neither objective nor subjective--in fact it is questionable whether those terms can be given any meaning--but it is clear that it is a fact in the concrete existence of individuals. It may still turn out that scientific inquiry cannot deal with values except as historical or biological facts, but if so, that is the result of the abstract character of the inquiry, not of the irrelevance or unimportance of value.

I cannot close without referring to Josiah Royce's great hope, for a community that encompasses us all, in a love that makes coercion unnecessary and exploitation impossible. I have no idea whether his hope will be fulfilled, or even whether it could be. We can take the first step, which, as he knew, is to see to it that we define ourselves and our communities not in terms of what we are against, but of what we are for.

COMMENT: Stephen White

In his paper "Values and Community," Professor Barnes' intention is to "sketch a general theory of the nature of value that may be of use to those who must find a way of restoring value to intellectual respectability" (p. 3). The most important source of this intellectual unrespectability has of course been what one might call the agenda of the great divide. This agenda has taken science to be the sole domain of reliable, systematic thinking. It is the domain of facts, reason, theory and the public testing of theory. On the other side of the great divide is the domain of value, of non-science. It is the domain of personal and ultimately non-rationally grounded judgments, including everything from taste in clothing and friends, to judgments about poetry and political systems.

The agenda of the great divide has been increasingly called into question in recent years. It is in the context of this questioning that Barnes wants to aid us in rethinking the role of value. This is certainly a worthy goal; however, I would like to raise a question about the appropriateness of starting toward such a goal by attempting to develop a general theory of value.

In taking up the task of providing a general account of the domain of value, it seems to me that Barnes is orienting his efforts at least partly in accordance with the agenda of the great divide. By this I mean that he has assumed that there is validity to thinking in terms of the domain of value. From the perspective of the great divide, this territory can be considered as one primarily because all sub-divisions (from taste in clothing to judgments about political systems) have the unifying characteristic of being non-scientific. Barnes also assumes this territory to be unified; however, he shifts the grounds for this assumption. The domain of value must be united by something more than the negative characteristic of being non-scientific; if this were not the case, one could not speak of a general theory of value. It is the existence of this "something more" that I wish to question. What I want to suggest is that the search for a general theory of value might encounter the same kind of problem as the search for a general theory of paganism--which begins with the assumption that there must have been something more that pagans had in common than merely their being non-Christian.

This example of a theory of paganism is admittedly extreme and perhaps overstates my point. The problem to which it draws attention, however, ought to be taken seriously. We should be aware of the degree to which the usage of the term "value" in contemporary philosophy has been molded by the agenda of the great divide. This fact becomes apparent if one consults the Oxford English Dictionary: "Value" has traditionally related to the worth of a thing, usually in an economic sense.[1] If this is the case, perhaps we should be quite cautious in assuming that the domain of value is something which lends itself easily to subsumption under a general theory.

Professor Barnes might respond to this line of criticism by saying that I should not take the concept of a general theory in such a strong sense, but rather see the domain of value as simply a subject matter about which useful generalizations can be made. For example, Barnes argues that value judgments have their primary function in critical dialogue; that they share the quality of fallibility; and that they should not be thought of as objective or subjective, but rather as irreducibly intersubjective. (pp. 3-5, 11)

Although I do in fact think that these generalizations have some validity, we should be aware that they raise a host of questions. I will mention only two. First of all, it might be argued that each of these generalizations applies not only to value judgments, but also to judgments about the truth or falsity of scientific theories. If this is so, then we need further generalizations which distinguish the latter sorts of judgments from the former. Second, it may be the case that the differences between types of value

---

[1] Cf. William K. Frankena, "Value and Valuation," The Encyclopedia of Philosophy (New York: Macmillan, 1967), pp. 229-32. Frankena suggests, correctly I think, that we might be advised to avoid the use of the term "value" whenever possible, "keeping to more traditional terms like 'good' and 'right,' which are better English."

judgments are at least as important as those similarities referred to by the generalizations. For example, judgments about the beauty of a painting and about the justness of capital punishment may both be fallible, but the significance of that fallibility for discourse and action is radically different.

Comment: Richard Lee

Professor Barnes' comments on value can be understood as part of the general movement in ethics away from metaethical questions, or questions about the meaning of ethical terms, to a fresh treatment of first-order moral questions. This trend became firmly established with the publication of Rawls' <u>A Theory of Justice</u> in 1971, and has now made itself felt in the upsurge of interest in medical ethics, business ethics, humanists who are hired by corporations and government agencies to give moral "input" as the phrase has it, and in teaching philosophy and ethics to third-graders. Despite some occasional foolishness, this trend is to be applauded, and hence I agree with Barnes when he says that "value has to come back." He does not mean that value has to come back in the sense that it really had gone away for awhile, for questions of value undergird every social practice, past and present. Rather, it has to return as a topic of conversation among men of sober intelligence, and shed its reputation as something which essentially escapes deliberate, rational, control and comprehension.

With these general sentiments, I agree. My questions concern some of the detail, in particular with what Barnes sees as a <u>theory</u> of the nature of value. A new spirit of talking about value may indeed be abroad in the land, in that the moral bearings of social practice are given more attention, but that does not settle the question of what a theory of value is.

Barnes seems to have two notions of what a theory is. The first is that a theory of value is an instrument whose own value is judged by its success in promoting and stabilizing other values. The second is that a theory of value is a description of and perhaps a clarification of those values that we do hold, but do not always hold reflectively. The success of a theory of this kind lies in its truthfulness, or accuracy. Whether these two conceptions are compatible is something I shall be examining in these brief remarks.

When he takes theory as an instrument Barnes tells us that he wants to sketch a theory of the nature of value that will be of use for those who want to restore value to intellectual respectability. He then mentions three conditions that such a theory will have to meet: it must prohibit inferences from 'ought' to 'is' (and perhaps from is to ought as well), it must declare invalid all claims to certainty about what is valuable, and it must require that the steps in a valid moral argument be somehow understood as historically ordered, and not ordered solely by the patterns of valid deductive or inductive reasoning. (This is how I construe his third assumption.) We do not yet know what the theory itself is, but let us suppose that it consists of arguments favoring those values that Barnes believes to be best or most fundamental. The content of the theory is therefore moral exhortation, in which the topics of individual life, communal aims, and social dialogue are given a central place. Our three conditions are then to be understood as an instruction about how we should go about exhorting people to adopt these principles of individuality, community, and dialogue. Let us then recast these constraints once again, and read them as advice given to the humanistic moralist: (1) don't make the mistake of being so kind to the world that you blind yourself to the obvious evil and declare instead that really, or secretly, or in the long run, this existing state of affairs is the best we could have, (2) remember that you could be wrong about any particular moral judgment you might make, and (3) in order to be effective, tailor your arguments to the actual condition of your audience, since you want to convert them and not simply entertain them.

If we follow these recommendations then Barnes believes that we may restore our first-order moral arguments to intellectual respectability. Is this in fact likely?

This is hard to say, largely because the concept of intellectual respectability is not very clear. The first recommendation expresses, I think, a perfectly sound moral opinion, and as a moralist I would urge that everyone adopt it, but I don't know if it would make moral argument more intellectually respectable or not. The second recommendation is one I would not make, nor do I think Barnes should make it. On many matters, of course, my moral judgment is fallible, but I am absolutely certain that there are many cases in which I judge correctly, and there is no good reason, least of all a morally good reason, why anyone should think I am wrong. I am absolutely certain that it would be wrong of me, right now and in these circumstances, to walk over to Professor Den Ouden and break his thumbs.

The last recommendation, though vague, is, I think, the best one. I read it as saying that when you moralize, do so with a keen awareness of the situation of your audience. Be rhetorically effective. Be sure to engage their interests, motivations, beliefs, and ideals. This will not guarantee good moral advice from you, but it will gain you some respect. However, it will do more to gain you moral respect than intellectual respect, but that is just fine. The problem with much of moral philosophy of the past few decades is that it was nothing if not intellectually respectable (as far as I understand that phrase)-- only it was not always morally respectable. It was, as Barnes suggests in several places, too abstract, too indifferent to the moral status of the moralist himself, and too much devoted to high-level questions of meaning. I think Barnes wants to say that questions of value are too important to be left to a certain kind of moral philosopher, and here I agree with him.

Axiology or the study of value conceived in this first way is then a success if in fact it produces more value, or at least conserves the old. But Barnes also suggests that a theory of value should be true to our experience and intuition, which may mean that a good value theory is a true value theory. What will make a value theory true will be, presumably, some relation it bears to our experience and intuition. I don't feel very certain about this, but I think that Barnes understands by "experience and intuition" something like the three conditions he calls the foundation of value. But whether that is exactly right or not is not the important thing at this point. I want to ask a question or two about the very notion of a true value theory.

I have suggested that a good value theory is one that espouses good things and right actions, and is an effective instrument in the hands of those who adopt the theory. Is anything left over for a true value theory? Perhaps if there were some values that were certain, important, and a source from which other values could be extracted, then we could call all the other values 'true' to the extent that they depended on these foundational values.

But this foundationalism does not accord very well with Barnes' fallibilism. The whole point of having a foundation in value theory or epistemology is that it protects you from wrong judgment. I don't see how Barnes is going to reconcile these two tendencies. But I, at least, have said that I am absolutely certain of some moral judgments. Why shouldn't I recommend some of them to Barnes? Or what is wrong with the ones he names, if he would be prepared to give up his fallibilism?

The difficulty is that the judgments which I know are the right ones do not take me very far. I know I should not break Den Ouden's thumbs, but should I ask him to loan me fifty dollars? I could use the money, no doubt about that. It is hard to say here: I probably should not. This is the trouble with all my moral certainties--they are far too jumbled and ramshackled to build even a respectable garden shed, much less an edifice fit for the family of man. And the trouble I find with Barnes' foundational values is that they give me precious little help when I need it most--should I ask for the fifty dollars? Is that a case of furthering individual life? Of being properly oriented toward communal aims? of keeping dialogue open? In short, Barnes' foundational beliefs are no doubt something you can build on, where mine are not; the problem is that one can build too many grand mansions on them. As far as I can see, Marx, Harry Truman, and Amy Semple McPherson could all have appealed to these principles. Barnes' underlying conditions turn out to be the foundations not of a mighty temple, but a Tower of Babel. (Of course I am being unfair to Barnes at this point--he can't say everything in ten pages. But I am trying to get your attention.)

The upshot of this is that I would urge that Barnes not worry about a true value theory. All he needs is a good one, and I have no doubt that that is what he will in fact produce.

PAPER II

ETHICS IN JOURNALISM

Theodore L. Glasser

Even the most superficial examination of the economics of contemporary American journalism will uncover a fundamental conflict between news as a journalistic ethic and profit as a business ethic, a conflict described by press critic Ben Bagdikian as the peculiar agony of a "godless corporation run for profit" and a "community institution operated for the public good."[1] My lecture today is an effort to examine the consequences of this conflict, particularly the journalist's growing disinterest in questions of right and wrong, good and bad.

My thesis, simply, is that the press has abandoned its commitment to a democratic society, and that any attempt to restore this commitment will require a radical departure from the principles of free enterprise and, in particular, a repudiation of the tenets of objective journalism. My thesis rests on the proposition that journalists today lack a discernible orientation, a frame of reference to which they might turn when faced with questions of value and quality. Typically, the owners of the daily press contend with--and respond to--economic imperatives alone, and thus what engulfs the profession is an occupational ethos which confuses editorial content *in* the public interest with editorial content *of* public interest.

Publishers today talk in terms of audiences, not communities; as entrepreneurs, they long ago abandoned civic boundaries in search of "retail trade zones" and "standard metropolitan statistical areas" and other territories ordinarily associated with marketing, not journalism. Publishers today seek to reach--ostensibly to serve--as large and as demographically attractive a readership as their circulation departments might conceive. To be sure, newspapers owners favor and fortify an industry whose chief commodity--the day's news--is prepared, packaged, and presented for purposes of profit maximization, not service to the com-

---

1 Ben H. Bagdikian, *The Effete Conspiracy* (New York: Harper & Row, 1972), p. 8.

munity.[2] Increasingly, publishers--and to a lesser extent their editors, reporters, and writers--have come to define the _value_ of news solely in terms of marketplace forces; _more_ often than not, the criteria used to assess press performance better reflect the publisher's economic welfare than any moral commitment to the aggregate social good.[3] Briefly and harshly, the standards used to guide individuals in their conduct as journalists are overwhelmingly self-serving, and as a consequence what prevails today is a largely _amoral_-- which is not to say _immoral_--view of the role of the press in society.

## JOURNALISM, AUTONOMY, AND THE LIBERTARIAN TRADITION

Historically and typically, journalists embrace a strictly libertarian interpretation of the First Amendment, a Constitutional perspective advanced long ago by those who saw the Bill of Rights as essentially protection for the rights and privileges of property owners. In the spirit of _laissez faire_, a libertarian view of journalism calls for an independent and wholly autonomous press, a press truly free to serve--and thus free to ignore--the interests and needs of its readers. On the question of responsibility or accountability, the libertarian journalist is clear: editorial self-determinism stands in opposition to "any attempt or pressure from outside journalism to provide some kind of 'common' or standard definition of journalistic

2   Otis Chandler of Times Mirror, which owns the Los Angeles _Times_, _Newsday_, and the Hartford _Courant_ among other media properties, recently explained the importance of an "attractive" readership, not merely a large readership: "We cut out unprofitable circulation . . . . The economics of American newspaper publishing is based on an advertising base, not a circulation base." Quoted in Ben Bagdikian, "When a Chain Adds a New Link," _The Bulletin of the American Society of Newspaper Editors_, February 1981, p. 36.

3   For a broader examination of whether the pursuit of profits can ever override otherwise obtaining moral considerations, see Alan H. Goldman, _The Moral Foundations of Professional Ethics_ (Totowa, NJ: Rowman & Littlefield, 1980), pp. 230-282.

responsibility to society."[4]

With the rise of the penny press in the mid-1800s, however, the quest for independence and autonomy began to manifest itself institutionally. If freedom of the press was once thought of as an individual liberty, it soon became reinterpreted to mean freedom for the press --clearly an institutional liberty. As newspapers and the newspaper industry began to resemble something more akin to a corporate empire than a great plurality of independent agencies of public communication, the press found itself able and certainly willing to define and defend itself as an institution--an institution of Constitutional significance. Thus, while editors, reporters, and writers became more and more accountable to publishers who were primarily concerned with circulation figures and advertising sales, publishers themselves joined forces--principally in the form of the American Newspaper Publishers Association--to resist any form of external control over their press. That is, while individual journalists lost much of their independence and autonomy, publishers began to expect for themselves all the privileges and immunities intended for "the press."

Although the judiciary has not entirely endorsed this kind of "institutional libertarianism," Justice Potter Stewart, in an address at Yale Law School in 1974, made clear his preference for a Fourth Estate, a fourth institution outside the Government created "as an additional check on the three official branches." As Justice Stewart understands it, the free press guarantee is a structural provision of the Constitution. "Most of the other provisions in the Bill of Rights," he explains, "protect liberties or specific rights of individuals: freedom of speech, freedom of worship, the right to counsel, the privilege against self-incrimination, to name a few. In contrast, the Free Press Clause extends protection to an institution. The Publishing business," Justice Stewart concludes, is "the only organized private business that is given explicit

---

[4] John C. Merrill, The Imperative of Freedom (New York: Hastings House, 1974), p. 204. Merrill's book is a defense of journalistic autonomy; his thesis is examined again in Existential Journalism (New York: Hastings House, 1977).

constitutional protection."[5]

As a structural provision, the guarantee of a free press not only isolates and insulates the press but at the same time bestows upon the press the awesome and unparalleled power to create and sustain public opinion. It is indeed a peculiarly optimistic provision, for unlike the executive, legislative, or judicial branches of government, the power of the Fourth Estate goes virtually unchecked. When, on occasion, the courts or Congress seek to challenge the press by holding it accountable for its actions, the press raises the banner of "freedom," invokes the "public's right to know," and plaintively cautions judges and legislators about their transgression and its inevitable "chilling effect" on the press. Even comparatively benign efforts to subject the press to public scrutiny--if not public accountability--have been met with suspicion and resistance. The National News Council serves well to illustrate the news media's unwillingness to accommodate a public forum for only discussion and debate on the performance of the press.

The National News Council was created in 1973 to "receive, to examine, and to report on complaints concerning the accuracy and fairness of news reporting in the United States, as well as to initiate studies and report on issues involving the freedom of the press."[6] Patterned after the British Press Council, which emerged in response to displeasure with British press performance after World War II, the National News Council depends on voluntary participation from the very press it tries to monitor. Like its counterpart in England, the Council has no enforcement power--only publicity. Nonetheless, the New York Times and the Washington Post refused to participate. Times publisher Arthur Ochs Sulzberger, in a memo to his staff, announced that the Times would not "furnish information or explanations to the council." Sulzberger feared that the council "would function as investigator,

5  For excerpts of Justice Stewart's speech, see "Or of the Press," Hastings Law Journal, 26 (January 1975): 631-637.

6  For background on the National News Council, see A Free and Responsive Press (New York: The Twentieth Century Fund, 1973).

prosecutor, and judge rolled into one."[7] For similar reasons, the New York Daily News described the Council as "a sneak attempt at press regulation, a bid for a role as unofficial news censor."[8]

Its opponents notwithstanding, the National News Council survives but, unhappily, must endure what William B. Arthur, its first executive director, calls the "ignominy of neglect"; for as Bagdikian recalls, the "history of publishers against the National News Council is a scandal."

NEWS, DEMOCRACY, AND THE MARKETPLACE METAPHOR

Since the early 1900s, when Oliver Wendell Holmes popularized the "marketplace of ideas" metaphor,[9] journalists have labored under the belief that a free press is a truly diverse and robust press, and that only a diverse and robust press can best serve the needs of a culturally plural society. Regrettably, the metaphor is more romantic than compelling, since there is no necessary connection between freedom of expression and diversity: "If the first amendment protects against the suppression of ideas, it follows that a market-place of sorts may emerge. It does not follow that a market-place will emerge or that if it does the result will seem fair or balanced." Clearly, a free

---

7  Quoted in Ronald P. Kriss, "The National News Council at Age One," Columbia Journalism Review, November/December 1974, p. 34.

8  Ibid. For a broader discussion on the lack of intellectually sound criticism of the press--and the press's resistance to criticism--see James W. Carey, "Journalism and Criticism: The Case of an Undeveloped Profession," The Review of Politics, 36 (April 1974): 227-249.

9  The "ultimate good desired," Justice Holmes argued, "is better reached by free trade in ideas--that the best test of truth is the power of the thought to get itself accepted in the competition of the market . . . ." See Abrams v. U.S., 250 U.S. 616 (1919).

press will not always yield a diverse marketplace.[10]

Still, as an economics metaphor rooted in a libertarian interpretation of the First Amendment, the "marketplace of ideas" retains its status as the principal justification for the existence of a press far more abundant, ironically, than it is diverse. Indeed, the marketplace metaphor is used today more literally than metaphorically--journalism's contribution to the marketplace is seen as valuable only as it proves to be profitable. Publishers are likely to argue that whatever sells well in the marketplace is, *ipso facto*, good for society, thus equating profitability with public service.

If anything, a free press tends to bring about a homogenized marketplace. Although the United States is richly abundant in newspapers and other media of communication, most Americans are trapped in what has been called a "no-choice informational bind," a condition endemic to mass communication.[11] Beyond the fact that fewer than five percent of the 1970 daily newspapers are in direct competition with another newspaper, most of the day's news is produced by a network or syndicate of one kind or another. Most newspapers today-- daily and weekly alike--serve as derivative "outlets" in that they derive their content from a handful of generative media.[12] A news story written for a particular community is the exception, not the rule;

10  See David L. Lange, "The Role of the Access Doctrine in the Regulation of the Mass Media," *North Carolina Law Review*, 52 (November 1973): 11. More generally see Bruce M. Owen, *Economics and Freedom of Expression* (Cambridge: Ballinger Pub. Co., 1975).

11  See Herbert I. Schiller, *The Mind Managers* (Boston: Beacon Press, 1973), p. 19. See also Hanno Hardt, "The Dilemma of Mass Communication: An Existential Point of View," *Philosophy and Rhetoric*, 5 (1972): 187.

12  "Derivative" and "generative" are terms used to denote a continuum of original newspaper content. See Thomas E. Patterson and Ronald P. Abeles, "Mass Communication Research and the 1976 Presidential Campaign," *Items* (Social Science Research Council), 2 (1975): 199-200.

usually, when journalists pursue an item of local interest they invest it with universal appeal, thus insuring a wide and profitable circulation--a circulation often enhanced by the wire services and other "wholesalers" of news.[13]

Paradoxically, it is less expensive for a newspaper to publish a story about, say, an earthquake in Italy than a story about corruption in the neighborhood police department. In large part, this is due to the advent of news wholesalers and the product they distribute: mass produced news. Not only are mass produced stories the least expensive to publish, but generally they are the most widely read. Even if the earthquake story is of no particular consequence to the reader, it stands out as a "good" story--the kind of story we read for much the same reason we watch a movie or read a novel.

In practice, this blurring of the distinction between news *in* the public interest--presumably a public service--and news merely *of* public interest gave rise to the widespread popularity of the human interest story. Beginning in 1835 with the New York *Sun's* "Moon Hoax," a celebrated but intentionally fictitious story about a species of "moon bat" that inhabited the moon (*vespertilo homo*, the story reported with an air of authenticity), the press became conspicuously aware of what kinds of stories sold the most newspapers. Moreover, it became abundantly evident to publishers that since the human interest story requires no local context, it could be purchased and published without having to be rewritten locally.[14]

With few exceptions, what appears on the front page of most daily newspapers is mass produced news; and what is appealing about mass produced news is its

13  For a discussion on the press's disregard for community, see Theodore L. Glasser, "The Aesthetics of News," *ETC.: A Review of General Semantics*, 37 (Fall 1980): 238-247.

14  For a history of the human interest story, see Helen MacGill Hughes, *News and the Human Interest Story* (New York: Greenwood Press, 1940).

human interest quality, not its vitality as information. Mass produced news may be important in some objective sense, but rarely does it impinge on the lives of most readers. For example, stories about international terrorism and distant disasters--two popular subjects among news wholesalers--may be intriguing and fun to read, but typically they do not provide readers with the vital information they need to adjust successfully to the world in which they live. Insofar as the marketplace is concerned, however, stories about international terrorism and distant disasters are of tremendous value to the publisher because (1) they attract large numbers of readers, and (2) they do not require a local and expensive editorial staff.

## OBJECTIVITY AND THE IDEOLOGY OF NEWS

To protect themselves in the marketplace, journalists needed a strategy, something to protect themselves from angry readers and upset advertisers, a tactic that could effectively deflect criticism and insure the newspaper's autonomy and independence. In response to this need emerged the conventions of objective reporting.[15]

Principally, there were two reasons for the introduction of objective reporting, an idea that came into vogue around the turn of the century. First, publishers found it financially unwise to offend readers (who often happened to be advertisers) with partisan views and fiery prose. The archtypical publisher in this instance was probably Adolph Ochs, whose New York Times adopted as its credo in 1896 an unprecedented pledge: "To give the news impartially without fear or favor, regardless of any party, sect or interest involved." The other reason had to do with emergence of news gathering cooperatives, most notably the Associated Press. Since these organizations had to service newspapers with diverse and often incompatible editorial politics, the news reports they distributed were

---

15 The conventions of objective reporting are operationally defined in Gaye Tuchman, "Objectivity as Strategic Ritual: An Examination of Newsmen's Notions of Objectivity, American Journal of Sociology, 77 (January 1972): 660-670.

necessarily limited to the "bare facts," with the opportunity for interpretation or analysis reserved for the individual client.[16]

Objectivity in journalism emerged not as a standard, however, but as a convention, the kind of organizational imperative to which Walter Lippmann referred when he called attention to the capricious and largely irrational enterprise of newsmaking.[17] Unlike standards, conventions do not provide a disciplined frame of reference for the journalist, a critical perspective from which reporters and editors might assess the quality of their performance or the value of their work. Instead, conventions provide routines: in the face of uncertainty, journalists need to know "how to proceed" and conventions--to the extent that they routinize newsmaking[18]--provide the necessary stability and decorum.

The peculiar thing about conventions, though, is that their present existence is often wholly unrelated to their origins. While objective reporting was as much as commercial imperative as anything else, it wasn't long before journalists rationalized it into a "canon of professional competence and an ideology of professional responsibility."[19] As early as 1924 Nelson Crawford, in his text on journalism ethics, expressly assumed that all journalists agreed with the basic tenets of objective reporting.[20]

---

16  For a concise history of objectivity in journalism, see Leon V. Sigal, Reporters and Officials (Lexington, Mass.: D.C. Heath & Co., 1973).

17  Walter Lippmann, Public Opinion (New York: Macmillan, 1965).

18  Gaye Tuchman, "Making News by Doing Work: Routinizing the Unexpected," American Journal of Sociology, 79 (July 1973): 110-131.

19  James W. Carey, "The Communications Revolution and the Professional Communicator," in P. Halmos (ed.), "The Sociology of Mass Media Communicators," The Sociological Review, 13 (January 1969): 33.

20  Nelson A. Crawford, The Ethics of Journalism (New York: Alfred A. Knopf, 1924).

By 1954 Louis Lyons, then curator for the Nieman Fellowship program for journalists at Harvard, was describing objectivity as a "rock-bottom" imperative: "Objectivity is the ultimate discipline in journalism. It is at the bottom of all sound reporting--indispensible as the core of the writer's capacity, of his integrity."[21] And in November 1973 the 30,000 members of the Society for Professional Journalists, Sigma Delta Chi, formally enshrined the idea of objectivity when they adopted as part of their "Code of Ethics" a paragraph characterizing objective reporting as an attainable goal and a standard of performance toward which journalists should strive.

Objectivity brought about fundamental changes in the role of the reporter. As the canons of objective reporting became more widespread, journalists were forced to relinquish their role as interpreter and analyst and became instead what Carey describes as a "professional communicator," a relatively passive link between sources and audiences:

> With the rise of "objective reporting" in the latter half of the 19th century, the journalist went through a process that can be fairly termed a "conversion downwards," a process whereby a role is deintellectualised and technicalised. Rather than an independent interpreter of events, the journalist became a reporter, a broker in symbols who mediated between audiences and institutions, particularly but not exclusively government. In this role he loses his independence and becomes part of the process of news transmission. In this role he does not principally utilize an intellectual skill as critic, interpreter and contemporary historian but a technical skill at writing, a capacity to translate the specialised language and purposes of government, science, art, medicine, finance into an idiom that can be understood by broader,

---

21 Louis M. Lyons, Reporting the News (Cambridge: Belknap Press, 1965), p. 295.

more amorphous, less educated audiences.[22]

To compensate for their lack of expertise, journalists began to rely more heavily on sources. Their skill as interviewers became more important than their ability to induce or otherwise engage in rational conjecture. Decidedly, sources and sources alone provide the sense and substance of the stories journalists tell. Sources supply the arguments, the rebutals, the explanations, and the criticism; sources puts forth the ideas while other sources challenge those ideas. Reporters, in their role as "professional communicators," merely provide a vehicle for these exchanges. As impartial observers journalists have neither the need nor the opportunity to develop a perspective from which to understand the events, issues, and personalities they were assigned to cover. While journalists are able to do a fine job reporting the facts truthfully, they are unable to assume responsibility for the truth about those facts.[23]

Just as objectivity in journalism brought about changes in the role of the reporter, the news, too, metamorphosed into something very different. News became something to be gathered, discovered, exposed-- an entity that existed independent of the journalist. News was no longer a story, a human creation, but something to be reported. And since journalists had little if any control over what constituted news, there was no apparent reason for journalists to accept responsibility for the day's news or, for that matter, its consequences for the reader. To be sure, the consequences of the day's news could only be of concern to journalists if they were willing to admit--to themselves if not the public at large--that the value or goodness of the news was their responsibility.

Walter Cronkite's view is perhaps typical of the prevailing attitude among journalists: "I don't think it is any of our business what the moral, political,

---

22  Carey, "The Communications Revolution and the Professional Communicator," p. 32.

23  For an early study of the probem between reporting the facts truthfully and reporting the fact about the truth, see Robert D. Leigh (ed.), A Free and Responsible Press (Chicago: University of Chicago Press, 1947).

social, or economic effect of our reporting is. I say let's go with the job of reporting--and let the chips fall where they may."[24] Consistent with Cronkite's view, a recent study of 29 editors of major metropolitan dailies found very little concern about the effect of media coverage on the growing incidence of terrorism. "Whether there is a causal connection between the amount of coverage and the increase of future assassination attempts, given the pattern of the assassin's need for notoriety," the study concluded, "is not a question pondered by the responding editors."[25] Indeed, a popular journalism text advises: "Valuable as the study of such factors as audience reaction may be for total understanding of social behavior, the first-rate newsgatherer acting as such persists in his search for truth. He does not ask himself what the potential use or effect of his information will be . . . . ."[26]

This lack of concern for the value of news not only underscores the meaning of objective reporting but explains, in part, why the practice of journalism today transcends questions of ethics. Clearly, if journalists are reluctant to decide what constitutes a _good_ news story, they will be even more reluctant to decide what constitutes _right_ conduct.

## FROM PROFESSIONAL TO ETHICAL JOURNALISM

What passes as ethics in journalism today is no more rigorous than the codes of ethics adopted by individual newspapers and professional societies. Such codes--which are often little more than "do's" and "don't's"--do little to promote standards of conduct consistent with the needs of the larger society. On the contrary, codes of ethics tend to insulate journalists by stipulating privileges peculiar to the profes-

24 Walter Cronkie, "What It's Like to Broadcast News," _Saturday Review_, December 1970, p. 53.

25 Harrell T. Allen and Richard J. Piland, "Bungling Assassins Rate Page One," _Journal of Communication_, 26 (1976): 101.

26 Curtis MacDougall, _Interpretative Reporting_ 7th ed. (New York: Macmillan, 1977), p. 11

sion. Journalists are not, therefore, instilled with a sense of duty and service to society but are rather engulfed by a sense of obligation to themselves. In Carey's view, this narrow concern for the well being of the profession is reflective of the growth of journalism ethics. Thus, Carey concludes, the "principal effect of professionalism is to erode the moral basis of society."[27]

To move beyond the narrow professionalism of today's journalism, and to begin to provide the foundation for what sociologist Alvin Gouldner calls a "grammar of rationality" for journalism, requires an intellectual commitment to the *idea* of news. What is needed is a critical theory of *news*, a coherent analysis of what news *ought* to be--not merely a study of what news *is*. As the basis for ethical conduct among journalists, there is a need for journalists to break away from what is *accepted* as news and to begin to wonder what is *acceptable* as news. What this means, in practice, is that questions of value--the good--must be dealt with before questions of ethics--the right--can be examined. In other words, journalists must know the value of news before they can determine the quality of their reporting.

Whether news is valuable or disvaluable, however, does not fall within the domain of ethics. Rather, value denotes good, and the relative value or disvalue of news is an empirical question, not a moral judgment. What *is* a question of ethics, though, is the journalist's struggle to bring about the good. Good news, it follows, is something journalists hope for and strive toward, whereas the right is something journalists must conform to. "The achievement of the good is desirable," the philosopher C.I. Lewis reminds us, "but conformity to the right is imperative."[28]

Following Lewis, for whom ethics and values fall into two distinct and yet inseparable camps, questions

---

[27] James W. Carey, "A Plea for the University Tradition," a paper presented to the Association for Education in Journalism, Seattle, August 13, 1978, p. 13.

[28] C.I. Lewis, The Ground and Nature of the Right (New York: Columbia University Press, 1955), p. 59.

of good necessarily precede and provide the foundation for questions of right. What is valuable is an empirical question in that it denotes the goodness or badness of an experience or an object--for present purposes the experience of reading a newspaper or the newspaper itself. What is ethical, however, is a moral judgment in that it specifies what must be done to bring about the good. Therefore, value is not a question of what is right but is a question of why something is right.

While the standards by which journalists might assess their conduct are, appropriately, a concern of ethics, these standards do not exist in a vacuum; they are rooted in the good, the valuable. Put another way, the validity of the distinction between right and wrong depends on a corresponding distinction between good and bad. A critical theory of news, then, requires an antecedent analysis of values, for as Lewis insists, "no action can be determined as right or wrong without reference to consequences of it as good or bad."[29]

Thus we return to the journalist's lack of concern for consequences (questions of value) and, by extention, the journalist's disinterest in right conduct (questions of ethics). To turn this around requires an analysis of values, and an analysis of values would begin with a series of four fundamental questions, listed here in descending order of abstraction:

       1. What is a good society?
       2. What is a good press system?
       3. What is a good newspaper?
       4. What is a good news story?

In the end, what news _ought_ to be is dependent on what a newspaper _ought_ to be; and what a newspaper _ought_ to be is dependent on what a press system _ought_ to be; and, finally, what a press system _ought_ to be is dependent on what society _ought_ to be. Once these questions have been answered, _then_ questions of ethics can be examined.

Ultimately, ethics in journalism should reflect what is good for society, not what is only good for journalism. And when professional and societal interests clash, it is essential that society call into

---

29  Ibid., p. 97

questions the values professions seek to promote. Accordingly, society--or at least its elected representatives--must examine the validity of the marketplace metaphor and assess the merits of an independent and autonomous press; it must identify and examine the value or values in which the ethic of objectivity is rooted. This is a task for society, not the press. For obvious reasons, publishers are not likely to build a case against their own industry.

COMMENT: George Michael Evica

I am in general and enthusiastic agreement with Ted Glasser's observations and judgments. I would like to comment on one apparent omission and on one definition, however.

Though Professor Glasser could point to his word "expose" as covering the omission (in his series "news ...is now something to be gathered, discovered, or exposed"), I think his phrases and words *objectivity*, *objective journalism*, and finally *mediate* all suggest he is focusing on what James P. Sisk has called "old-style objective reporting." Sisk has stated it succinctly in a review-article[1] on Tom Wicker's book On Press:

> The real story in [Wicker's] On Press is the process by which...old-style objective reporting gave way to investigative journalism and "the new adversary approach." (49)

Now, the investigatory methodology, the techniques and strategies, of the investigative journalist is *not* new, since it is the "reemergence of the muckraking tradition." (49) What is new--or what is apparently new--is the adversarial posture of the investigative journalist. But one could argue that the role of adversary played by the reporter as against his source brings subjectivity back *into* journalism. Possibly: at

---

[1] James P. Sisk, "All the News that Fits the Story," Worldview (November, 1978) p. 49-52. Further references to this article will be made parenthetically within the body of the text. See also Hayden White, Metahistory (Baltimore: Johns Hopkins Press, 1973), and The Writing of History [:] Literary Form and Historical Understanding, eds. Robert H. Canary and Henry Kozicki (Madison, Wisconsin: The University of Wisconsin Press, 1978). Though Sisk fully appreciates the value of Northrop Frye's critical theory to journalistic plot lines, he does not seem aware of Hayden White's application of Frye to historiography; in turn, the essayists in The Writing of History do not seem to know of Sisk's short but important essay.

least the proposition needs to be explored. In any event, discussion of so-called "objectivity," "professional communicators," and "technicians who mediate between sources and audiences" in Glasser's presentation needs to be modified--or at least extended--to include adversarial, apparently non-objective, investigatory reporting. Especially since questions of good and bad ought to be answered prior to questions of right and wrong in this hell-raising type of journalism and are possibly even more pressing in the "new" than in the "old." Neither the "old-style" objective mode nor the "new" investigatory mode seems able to, as Glasser put it, "report the truth about the facts."

And that inability is precisely a function of journalism's valuing behavior. I would like to comment, therefore, on one definition. Quoting Glasser: "Value refers to the consequences of conduct..." I would start valuing behavior earlier than the measuring of consequences. Briefly, I take valuing to be the positive or negative valencing, preferences or aversions, the potential attraction or repulsion, of an anticipated recurrence as it seems to appear again in measured--time-factored--human experience. Measuring human eventing ultimately means, for example, anticipating spring, growth, fecundity, remembering winter, waste, and barrenness, and establishing inductive types of needs and types of dreads, romantic and ironic polarities which build our genres, our typologies, our models of rite, ritual, myth, and literature. Valuing in this sense leads to story-telling.

How does this genre-building, this story-telling, affect journalism, the values of journalism, and finally the ethics of journalism? Glasser gives us a lead: "...news was once a human creation, like the novel or the poem." Again, following Glasser, we can ask a crucial question: what constitutes a good news story? Or, shifting our emphasis, what constitutes a good news story? The most insidious, value-denying or value-destroying dimension of both kinds of journalism is what has been called the "story trap." "The 'story trap' is the misuse of those patterns of fiction that everyone employs [often unknowingly, primitively, or naively ] to give significant shape to information." (50) We must recognize in all reporting the "extent to which the validation of information depends on story form" (50: emphasis added)--on the time-factored, narrative mythos of the story. Even among educated jour-

34

nalists "few...have been forced to consider all the ramifications of the basically [ fictive ] ...nature of their enterprise." (50) Journalists are hence in no position to examine their own "responsibility" or "accountability" at the "deep-structure" level of their discourse. They therefore need to read and to study and consume "books like Wayne Booth's Rhetoric of Fiction, Frank Kermode's A Sense of an Ending, ... Northrop Frye's Anatomy of Criticism , [ Kenneth Burke's Motives series, and Hayden White's Metahistory ]." (50)

>[Objective reporting] ...deals in contexts of so-called "facts" organized in familiar story patterns by relatively faceless organizers to make the contexts intelligible and interesting, the patterns themselves being for the most part so well established [as declined or secularized myths] in the public mind that they are prime determinants of newsworthiness... (50: emphasis added)

Hence those patterns function as value assessers--the parameters of value--of what is to be written, how it is to be written, and whether it is to be published at all:

>...the world as we perceive it, and as [journalists] ...report it, is not mere sequences of events but events structured, or plotted, into significant patterns, and the plots or patterns are the same ones that structure our [rituals, myths, epics, legends, dramas, tales, and] stories." (50)

If then--value or at least value-processing--is to be our central concern in journalism, so that the "quality of [its] conduct" can be attended to, it must be the duty of the reporter to distinguish among archetypal, recurrent and value-rich plots, rejecting the obsessive, over-worked, value-weakened plots that currently dominate our journalism from the New York Post to the Washington Post. Thus what Sisk calls "the grossness of the plots" found in our daily newspapers (whether sensationalist or sober) "both determines and ...[is] served by the selection of information." (50) Public hunger for "victimization, conspiracy, happy-ending, and expose" story-lines is fed by the daily press which in turn "debases these plots for serious use." (50) Those individuals and groups responsible for "the gathering, processing, and publishing of information" must be made aware that

> ...we will probably continue to rely on that repertory of marvelously efficient (if often distorting) information-processing machines constituted by our fictions [,] ...familiar plot patterns in our fables, legends, myths, midrashim, and metaphors ... [,] not ultimately to discard this repertory and possess the plain truth [whatever that truth is] at last, but to refine it." (51)

Caught in this debasing trap of the "story"--and without the value-enhancing options of the great narrative proto-patterns--to be learned only from our sacred texts, our myths, and our literatures--both the objective reporter and the investigative journalist are incapable of either examining "questions of value" or "questions of ethics."

COMMENT: Stephen Norland

Professor Glasser's essay points successfully to some organizational and economic elements responsible for the decline of journalism in the public interest. With economic stability never guaranteed, market forces may indeed lead to an over-concern with business success at the expense of reporting in the people's best interest. Also, his analysis is provocative in suggesting that the ethic of objectivity serves this end. In becoming only transmitters of information journalists abandon their interpretive and analytic role. To be able to evaluate news reporting as ethical or as unethical first requires a specification of what is good for society, as opposed to what is only beneficial for the news business. Professor Glasser argues, "questions of good necessarily precede and provide the foundation for questions of right." There are intriguing issues lodged in those recommendations which deserve further exploration.

First, it is extremely difficult to specify what the needs of a society are. Even for one which claims to be politically democratic, it may be misleading to talk of one society with a clearly specifiable set of requirements. Contemporary United States is heterogenous; the various groups and segments of the society hold many conflicting interests which cannot all be served in the same way.

Is it any less difficult to determine what the role of the press should be under those conditions? Considerable attention is paid to the role of the press in a democratic society as being the watchdog of the officially constituted branches of government, a Fourth Estate in Justice Stewart's terms. Yet any institutional segment of society placed in a seemingly advantaged position by government officials is likely to be a timid guardian. It would indeed be a scoop if an industry which is beholden to government for its priviledged status checks that government too tightly. To the extent that members of the press system enjoy a special relationship to government, can we anticipate that the former will jeopardize that arrangement by holding members of the latter accountable for abuses?

Rather than constituting a watchdog of governmental

power, many press-government relationships take on elements of ritualistic deference to the power of government and its officials. Government officials substantially control what information exists for journalists to transmit to the public. Maintaining a small amount of access leads to the tendency to ease even the marginal amount of pressure now exerted to determine the truth about the facts. When the questioning gets tough, officials can withdraw, respond with the popular "no comment," or, as a recent governor did, refuse to answer any more "negative" questions. The current structural inequality characteristic of the government-press relationships exerts pressure to not question the truth about the facts.

Political power of government is only one aspect of the structural relationships bringing about a benign press. As Hess (1981)[1] recently argued, news about how many government programs operate requires reporters to penetrate the federal bureaucracy for their stories. Not only is this less interesting for reporters, but they also encounter organizational barriers to information characteristic of bureaucracies. Increasingly perhaps, gathering information necessitates imposing on bureaucratic organizations to gather material for news stories. This poses a set of special problems for reporters, which complement Glasser's analysis of the economic pressures on news businesses.

Max Weber (1946)[2] noted that secrecy is an important dimension of a bureaucratic organization's relationship to the other segments of society. Both public and private bureaucracies seek to control access to information about their operations and to shield their activities from public scrutiny. Control over information--a resource in today's world--thus increases a bureaucrat's and a bureaucracy's power. Reporters are thus dependent on bureaucrats for access to key information.

1  Stephen Hess, "Rating Washington Press," *Hartford Courant* (Thursday, June 25, 1981), p. A25.

2  Max Weber, "Bureaucracy," pp. 196-244 in H.H. Gerth and C. Wright Mill (eds.) *From Max Weber: Essays in Sociology*. (New York: Oxford University Press, 1946).

Consequently, reporters find themselves dependent on authorities for their information. They become passive transmitters of information, in Glasser's terms. It is probable that the information derived from these sources is self-serving to the organization rather than to the other segments of society when those interests conflict. To be in a position to be ethical, or to report a truth about the facts, requires reporters to establish extraordinary relationships. Because they are relatively unusual they are not strengthened by the typical institutional bases of support. They are relatively marginal to the established press system.

Sjoberg and Miller (1973)[3] identify several modes of adversary reporting. To one extent or another, they all conflict with our current press system. Note also that the individual reporters are not unaccustomed to a critical stance toward their subject matter. One may, as I.F. Stone, develop one's own constituency so that exchange of favors with bureaucrats is unnecessary. By relying on written records reciprocity with bureaucrats is avoided. Another model is based on social contacts established and cultivated over a long period of time and is illustrated by the work of Seymore Hersh. It would hardly be compatible with meeting tomorrow's deadline. Information of the kind which bureaucratic relationships tend to keep secret can be obtained from disgruntled insiders or from those with a questionable reputation. These persons are unlikely to stand behind the microphones for public press conferences. With these kinds of sources, however, reporters run the risk of discredit from those arguing a different point of view. Nevertheless, Jack Anderson is able to pursue his critical stance by employing these methods. On occasion it is possible to develop alliances with some members of the bureaucracy or governmental elite (but not without some reciprocity) in order to obtain material that lay behind the publicized facts, as is the case with the Nader group. While some of these styles are related to the current press system, to different degrees they involve relationships which conflict with that organization. In addition then to the economic elements that concern Glasser, structural characteristics of bureaucracy and government inhibit the extent

3  Gideon Sjoberg and Paula Jean Miller, "Social research on bureaucracy: limitations and opportunities," Social Problems 21 (Summer 1973), 129-43.

to which reporters can report a truth about the facts.

A different kind of issue is raised by Glasser's linkage of ethical conduct with the good society. He suggests that news reporting cannot be evaluated as ethical or as unethical without taking into account the consequences of the story. Glasser's argument is uncertain in two respects that I want to mention. First, it links the ends or consequences for society with the means--the reporter's action. Can or should the ends of action always determine the moral correctness of that action? It is not clear that the consequences for some audience are not in part determined by the means. People do, it seems to me, judge the impact of things in part on how they were done. The impact of efforts also are assessed on the basis of the reputation of the person doing the work. It is difficult at times to separate the means and ends of actions in the way that Glasser does. In a society marked by substantial inequality, where everyone does not enjoy the same opportunity to be consequential, is this linkage desirable?

This contingency points toward the second difficulty with the perspective suggested by Professor Glasser. The significance of a piece of journalism and its consequences are not objective characteristics of the effort, but are to a large extent outcomes of negotiation, revision and reconsideration. The consequences of journalistic work depend on how various people respond to it, including other journalists, government officials and citizens. Assuming this is so, the linkage of consequences with ethics seems to imply that journalists will be ethically accountable in large part on the basis of how others respond to their work. And, as Glasser acknowledges, some consequences of actions are ambiguous and uncertain at the time when the work is undertaken. Does an uncertain outcome provide sufficiently clear guides for how specific actions are performed?

A concern for how stories are written, however, needs to be distinguished from how a story is selected to be written in assessing the linkage between reporting and its social consequences. Questions of ethics in reporting need to encorporate both how a story is constructed and what stories are written. Although the data are mixed, some research indicates that public anxiety about crime may be more related to news coverage than what is justified by police statistics or personal experiences (Conklin, 1975:[4] McIntyre, 1975[5]). If media have become theatre (Lapham, 1981a[6]), then Glasser squarely points to a significant connection between what dramas are featured and their impact on the audience.

Contrary to some observers of the journalistic world (i.e., (Lapham, 1981b[7]) who see no journalistic responsibility to separate worthless information from the important, the complexity and rapid pace of today's world require a framework to do just what Glasser recommends: to determine the value and quality of reporting. If we have only a limited amount of time--and energy--to participate in the process of informing ourselves then it is not unimportant that a lot of news is distracting. Imbedding a story in a mass of diversions does not benefit segments of the public. Professor Glasser's argument for a reconsideration of the relationships among stories, newspapers, the press system and the world we inhabit is a welcomed call. His suggestion that we all participate in identifying frames of reference from which to judge the quality and value of journalists' work is also an important initial step in the process of defining responsibility in this consequential segment of our society.


4   John E. Conklin, <u>The Impact of Crime</u>  (New York: Macmillan, 1975).

5   Jennie McIntyre, "Public attitudes toward crime and law enforcement," pp. 185-203 in Richard L. Henshel and Robert A. Silverman (eds.), <u>Perception in Criminology</u>  (New York: Columbia University Press, 1975).

6   Lewis H. Lapham, "Gilding the news," <u>Harper's</u>  (Vol. 263, No. 1574; July 1981a), p. 31-39.

7   Lewis H. Lapham, "Sculptures in snow," <u>Harper's</u> Vol. 263, No. 1575; August 1981b), p. 8-11.

PAPER III

LIFE AND ART

Jonathan Bushnell Bakker

In this paper I shall argue that if we accept the idea that there are no limits on what can be a medium for a work of art, then we shall have to revise radically our ideas about the relation of art to the rest of our lives. Given that the relation of art to life has come into question, I argue that the distinction between evaluating art and evaluating life also comes into question. I then argue that the moral criteria commonly used in evaluating life's activities and the aesthetic criteria used in evaluating art actually overlap.

In recent years the notion that anything can be used as a medium in creating a work of art has found increasing acceptance within the art world. Restrictive ideas about what materials constitute the proper media for works of art have begun to weaken. There are fewer and fewer constraints operating on artists as to what they can use as their medium to make an artwork. I will mention only a few randomly selected examples: Rauschenberg's "combines", "junk" metal sculpture, "soft" sculpture, any example of conceptual, performance, or body artworks, Andre's rocks here in Hartford, Christo's works, and, in music, Cage's and Stockhausen's work. All of these artists, movements, or types of art share a radical departure from a tradition which jealously guarded certain particular media as the only legitimate media in which to create a work of art. It has taken quite a long time for lithography and photography to be accepted as legitimate media, but it seems that they are now accepted.

Though there is wide acceptance within the artworld of the notion that we cannot impose constraints on media, I acknowledge that such acceptance outside a relatively elite circle is probably small. Therefore we must begin by asking, "What is a medium?" In traditional art forms we generally mean by the medium the materials which the artist used in making the work of art. Thus sculptures have as their medium bronze or marble and paintings have as their medium oil, or acrylic, or water color paint on some particular kind of surface (wood, stretched canvas, paper). I cannot discover any reasons for regarding traditional media as having any privileged status except that they have been in use for quite some time, which only means that somebody, a very long time ago, <u>started</u> using these media and others have followed suit. But if all it took to have paint, for example, accepted as a medium was to have someone start using it successfully, then anyone could start using anything as a medium successfully, and it should be accepted. Do we really want to say that it is too late to start a new medium? What was special about the old days? Do we want to say that a certain number of years must go by after a new material is used to make an artwork before that material is a legitimate medium? What is it in the meanwhile? It looks, then, as though limitations on medium are mainly, if not entirely, based on a tradition of innovation which we have no good reason to think has ever ended. If it has not ended then it is still ongoing and artists must still be allowed to begin to use new materials as their medium. I am not denying here the importance and value of tradition. It could be the case that traditional media are the best available--though what this might mean is not clear. The point here is only that good artists require the freedom to <u>extend</u> the tradition they inherit.

A slightly more theoretical consideration in favor of the notion that there cannot be constraints on medium is contained in the following question: How is an individual medium to be identified? We frequently see the expression "mixed medium" on an identifying tag next to some artwork in a gallery. But what is to prevent someone from saying that some <u>collection</u> of materials is her medium? Is the medium of dance really movement, or is it movement and costume and story, etc.? Is this a combination of different media or one medium? If it is a combination of media, how <u>many</u> media are there and how do we individuate them? Would it not make more sense to say, in some cases, that <u>the</u> medium of a given work of art is a complex of <u>elements</u> which in other cases may be regarded as individual media? What I am suggesting is that what we regard as a medium might be relative to a given situation. If it is not clear how to identify an individual medium, we might as well admit that it is either a relative or an arbitrary notion. After all, the "medium" of oil paint consists of many <u>different</u> colors of oil paint, frequently applied with many different instruments (brushes of all sorts, palette knives, fingers, etc.) and in different consistencies (thick and pasty, thin and watery). Why should each of these possible variations not be regarded as distinct media? There may be better reasons for regarding the way de Kooning, Frankenthaler, and Poussin apply oil paints as distinct media than there are for regarding acrylics and oils as distinct media. It is easy to imagine a tag next to a painting in a gallery reading: "Medium: thick oil paint applied with palette knife and paint brush handle."

In summary, then, limits on what is regarded as a proper medium are completely arbitrary, i.e., mistakenly derived from a tradition of innovation that extends up into the present. Further, the concept of a medium is itself so unclear that it is impossible to say how one medium can be distinguished from another. Given that we do not know how to distinguish one medium from another, we are not in a position to deny someone the right to call a particular material or collection of materials her medium. (I have spoken of "materials" in this discussion for convenience only; obviously, I do not mean to imply that such things as events, actions, concepts, etc., could not also be media for a work of art.)

If anything can be a medium, if there are really no limits on what can be used as a medium to create a work of art, then it is possible that many things we don't usually consider to be media could be used as media. Why could not running for political office be done as work of art? Brushing one's teeth? Breathing? Driving a bus? Giving a philosophy lecture? (Rich Gold, a contemporary composer, actually does give "concerts" which consist of lectures on the nature of art.) If anything can be a medium, then we cannot exclude all the sorts of activities that we normally regard as "practical", as having to do with "life", as potential media for works of art. Washing dishes could be done as a work of art. In fact, life itself seems to become one of the possible media for creating a work of art. What is to prevent someone from saying, "My entire life, every aspect of it, is my work of art. I will make my statement by living in a particular way. I will include every aspect of the way I feel, think, move, talk, etc." If anything can be a medium, then this seems to be a permissible move.

Conceptual artists and performance artists are artists who have recognized the truth of something like what I am arguing here. Thus, writing an essay on aesthetics, shipping artworks from one museum to another, and shaking hands with all the sanitation workers in New York City have all been "done" as works of art. But I want to take this argument beyond where it has been taken (to my knowledge) by any of these individuals. These artists, it seems to me, have understood that any of the activities that are normally regarded as "practical" activities, such as washing dishes, could be used as media for the creation of a work of art. But, for the most part, they have hesitated in the face of drawing the ultimate conclusion from this line of thinking. There is a further step that remains to be taken.

These artists have continued to treat the works of art that they create using these relatively novel media as constituting some kind of an island in their lives, as some kind of excerpt from their lives. In this specific sense, they have not changed the traditional way of approaching art and artworks. These artists continue to create objects (or events, performances, etc.) which stand apart from them as individual persons, however much those objects may affect them as persons. One's life is, in this sort of case, still regarded as space to which one retreats from the artwork. Even if one does go to the studio to explore one's life, the remainder of one's life is still regarded as a place to which one can escape from one's art. The artwork is treated as something basically separate from one's life. If it seems that the possibility of there not being any escape from one's art could create a claustrophobic atmosphere, I think this is entirely possible--though not necessary. It could be that this sort of claustrophobia contributed to the suicides of people like Van Gogh, Rothko, and David Smith; perhaps, tragically, it finally seemed to them that the only escape remaining to them was death.

The possibility I am arguing for here is the possibility of an artist's erasing the distinction between art and life altogether. That this is a possibility seems to follow directly from the admission that there are no limits on what can count as a medium. If anything can be a medium, then life itself could be a medium. Since our lives involve an indefinite number of aspects this would obviously be a project of gargantuan proportions. Perhaps a project of this sort would be doomed to failure, or at least to result in bad art. On the other hand, perhaps not.

    Several well-known artists have made comments which indicate that they are aware, to some extent, of the possibility of a life of art. Duchamp, for example, remarked in an interview, "Therefore if you wish, my art would be that of living: each second, each breath is a work which is inscribed nowhere, which is neither visual nor cerebral."[1] In the same interview he says that it is important to consider the artist as a medium. Rauschenberg commented one time, "I'd really like to think that the artist could be just another kind of material in the picture, working in collaboration with all the other materials."[2] Rauschenberg did go on to say that he did not think this was really possible. In any case, there are hints that some artists have considered the possibility of what I am suggesting, that an artist could take his or her life as the medium for an artwork. This possibility is what I have called "the life of art."

    I have been arguing that since there are no limits on what can be used as a medium to make a work of art, an artist could choose to take his or her life as the medium for a work of art. That marble can be used to make a work of art would not lead anyone to think that some unquarried, uncarved marble was an artwork; nor is the paint job on someone's house a work of art simply because it is done in oil paint. That a given kind of stuff could be used as a medium to create a work of art does not imply that it ever actually has been so used or that any particular sample of it has been so used. The point here is that there is obviously more involved in what a work of art is than what it is made out of. Poems are made with language, but this would not lead anyone to think that, therefore, newspapers must be artworks. That a life could be an

---

1  Marcel Duchamp, "Art as Non-Aesthetic: I Like Breathing Better than Working," in *Aesthetics: A Critical Anthology*, eds. George Dickie and R.J. Sclafani (New York: St. Martin's Press, 1977), p. 543.

2  Calvin Tompkins, *The Bridge and the Bachelors* (New York: Penguin Books, 1976), p. 232.

artwork does not imply that any life is (or ever will be) an artwork. It should be clear that I am not arguing that we can no longer, in general, make the distinction between art and life; the position I am taking is only that there exists the possibility that in some case (or cases) we may no longer be able to make the distinction.

The general problem of the definition of art (and the criteria that determine what is and what is not art) is a very difficult issue that is independent of the question being discussed here. Whether or not a given life were a work of art (and, for that matter, whether it were a good, bad, or indifferent one) would be determined in the same ways that would be applicable to any other case. Form, content, structure, style, meaning, intention, attitude, context, and potential for appreciation have all, at various times, been considered essential to a thing's being a work of art. Whether some or all of these are essential properties of a work of art is the question of the definition of a work of art, a question that has been central in both art and philosophy of art in this century. It seems clear that if the multitude of things we presently regard as artwork can have whatever properties we regard as essential, then a life could also have those properties. Whether, in fact, any life has (or ever will have) the requisite properties, and whether, as a result, that life is a good, bad, or indifferent work of art, remains an open question.[3]

We ordinarily apply pragmatic and moral considerations in evaluating both our own daily actions and those of others. Whether discussing political, domestic, or business activity we bring these practical and moral considerations to bear with an unquestioning sense of their relevance. We also generally recognize that it is <u>aesthetic</u> considerations, rather than practical or moral considerations, that apply in evaluating works of art. That a painting serves no so-called "practical" purpose is not usually considered a valid criticism. Likewise, in most cases, moral considerations would not be thought appropriate in evaluating an artwork (though clearly there are exceptions). Thus,

---

3   I am indebted to Sherry Buckberrough and Cris Horton for convincing me that I needed to clarify this issue.

we generally apply very different criteria of evaluation to things considered to be parts of our lives, on the one hand, and to works of art, on the other hand.

If the very same action can be performed both as a practical activity in one's life and as a creative work of art, then how are we to tell the difference between art and life? Indeed, what becomes of the distinction between art and life? We generally think of art and life as constituting quite distinct realms. When we understand the implications of the notion that anything can be a medium, we see that it raises a <u>radical</u> question about what art <u>is</u>, about the nature of <u>art</u>. If life itself can be a work of art, then what is left to distinguish art and life? What <u>is</u> art? Depending on what art turns out to be, it may be the case that certain people are already performing their practical tasks as works of art--perhaps even unbeknownst to <u>them</u>. And, on the other hand, it seems that it could turn out that many of the things we currently regard as works of art will turn out <u>not</u> to be works of art once (or, if) this question about the nature of art is resolved.

It may seem odd to some to suggest that an artwork could be created by someone without his knowing that he had done so. It could be argued that both the specific intention to create an artwork and a certain cultural and theoretical context are required before a genuine work of art can come into existence. I have already argued that the exact definition of art is an independent question, and that whether a given life were a work of art would be decided in exactly the same ways applicable to other objects and events. Nevertheless, this is an important issue, and the following points deserve to be mentioned. To begin with, two counterexamples immediately come to mind: found art and artworks created by accident (chance) are accepted as art though the "proper" intention was obviously not present. Once displayed in a gallery these things would have the proper context; but it remains true that they were not created as works of art. One could argue that "recognizing" these objects as artworks is equivalent to creating them with aesthetic intention, but this begins to sound artificial. In any case, the second point I wish to make is decisive. Before moving on to this second point, it is worth mentioning that many of the objects we regard as great art were created by skilled artificers (artisans) who lacked the very concept of art--Greek vases and African masks, for example.

The second answer I wish to make to this objection is this: it may be that, in fact, the "proper" intention is present in a case in which an artwork is created unawares, though that intention is understood under a different description. Consider the following case. Suppose a folk artist somewhere in the hills enjoys painting pieces of wood to make them look like watermelon slices. This modest person would never <u>dream</u> of treating his artifacts as falling into the same category as objects created by wealthy big-city artists--he only makes them because he thoroughly enjoys making them and because he thinks they are "nice" when completed (not to mention that his friends like them). Does this folk artist's modesty and ignorance of big-city art theory really prevent his watermelon slices from becoming art? His intentions may be, in fact, very similar to those of many big-city artists associated with prestigious galleries and museums. Though his intentions (and his context) would be different in detail, it could be that this folk artist does have the kind of intentions necessary to classify his artifacts as artworks. The point here is that essentially the same feelings, attitudes and beliefs may be present in two different persons, though those persons would describe them differently as a result of differences in their particular lives.

If there is a question about how to distinguish art from life, a practical activity from a creative (aesthetic) one, then there is also a question about how to evaluate these actions and their results. We generally apply moral considerations to people's <u>lives</u> and aesthetic considerations to the artworks they <u>produce</u>. In fact, we generally regard moral standards as being higher, in some sense, than aesthetic standards, such that if there were a conflict between them we would expect a person to perform the moral act as opposed to the aesthetic one. But if the distinction between their lives and their artworks has broken down, then the foundation for distinguishing between moral values and aesthetic values has also broken down. If this is so, how are we to judge and evaluate a life that is supposed to be a work of art, or that is admitted to be a work of art?

The notion that anything can be a medium, then, has far-reaching consequences. It leads to the possibility that a life could be a medium for a work of art, and thus, to a question about the difference between art and life. This in turn raises a question about the very nature of art. Finally, if the distinction between art and life is blurred, then the distinction between moral and aesthetic standards of evaluation also seems to be blurred.

We are now faced with the question, what standards of value, of judgment, apply to a life that is a work of art? Given an action that is "practical" and is supposed to be a work of art, are we to apply moral criteria or aesthetic criteria in evaluating that action? Perhaps we could begin to answer this question if we could find some common ground between moral and aesthetic standards of value. If it turned out that aesthetic and moral standards overlapped at some fundamental level, this would contribute significantly to resolving the question. Should this be the case, then, in at least some cases, there would be no conflict: the moral and aesthetic judgments would yield the same result.

It is common to distinguish between things that are valuable for their own sakes and things that are only valuable for their consequences. I value smelling cognac simply as good in itself and not for any good consequences; I value surgery for its consequences and not in itself. Many people would agree that a fundamental principle of morality is the principle that all persons, simply because they are human beings, should be treated with equal respect because they are valuable purely for their own sakes. The foundation for the possibility of treating others equally is the capacity we have for recognizing that some things are good in themselves. When I smell a good cognac there is a flash of appreciation which involves a recognition that the existence of such an experience is good _irrespective of who is having it_. Such an experience is good in itself; it is simply good that experience of this kind should _exist_. This sort of appreciation is true of many kinds of human experience. When we become clear about the nature of such appreciation, then we discover that we have a duty of some sort to show respect even for the potential for such experience. Since I recognize that other human beings either have such experiences or are capable of such experiences, I recognize that each person is worthwhile, is good, just because of the kind of thing he or she is. A person does not have to be good for anything to be good. A person is the kind of thing that is good in itself, for its own sake, as an end rather than as a means to some consequences. The foundation of this kind of evaluation is our capacity to appreciate a thing's intrinsic worth, to recognize that it is good simply that a certain kind of thing exists. If we did not have this kind of appreciation we probably would never know that there were things good in themselves; we would be limited to recognizing mere instrumental goodness.

I take what I have been saying to be roughly similar to Kant's moral theory. One way to explain Kant's position would be to say that an action is right if it is done out of some sense of appreciation of the intrinsic value of any person as an end in himself or herself. In slightly more technical language, the good will is the foundation of all moral values and, only that will is good which strives to take as its sufficient motive for an action the sense of reverence or respect we naturally feel when we become aware of the moral law, the categorical imperative. A deep and sensitive awareness of the categorical imperative "naturally" produces in us a sense of appreciation of the value of other persons as ends in themselves. Though our interests and desires frequently incline us toward actions that would not be done out of our sense of duty, we are capable, because we are rational beings, of being motivated purely out of our "transcendental" appreciation of the value of rational beings as ends in themselves. A good will is one which always strives to take this kind or appreciation as the sufficient motive for its actions.[4]

The appreciation of persons for their own sakes then, is an important moral principle. I have used the term "appreciation" in an intuitive way until now. One

---

[4] In my interpretation of Kant, I am indebted to the following article: Paul Dietrichson, "What Does Kant Mean by 'Acting from Duty'?", in Kant: A Collection of Critical Essays, Robert Paul Wolff, ed. (Garden City: Anchor Books, 1967).

dictionary definition of the term is "sensitive awareness; especially recognition of aesthetic values." "Sensitive awareness" comes very close to what I mean by "appreciation", but I would not restrict its use to aesthetics. It is through something like sensitive awareness of our status as rational beings that we develop a sense of obligation to treat others equally.

Now the arts are also thought to involve appreciation, and, again, what we mean is something like sensitive awareness. Indeed, there are courses taught in "art appreciation"; presumably what is taught in these courses is some kind of sensitivity to what is going on in artworks (or, at least, what is going on in artworks is taught in the hope that some sensitivity will develop). It is interesting to note here that, according to the 1980 yearbook of the University of Hartford, "The Hartford Art School cultivates the appreciation of all things as art . . . ."

I hardly need mention that there is a long tradition in the arts according to which art is not valuable as a means to anything; art is simply valuable for its own sake, as an end in itself.[5] Thus, in art, as in morals, our capacity to appreciate something for its own sake, as an end in itself, turns out to be a foundational value. We could say that art is a discipline whose task it is to make and recognize things which are good in themselves. So art is a practice in which the special kind of appreciation that is fundamental to morality is cultivated. What is it that we appreciate in an artwork? This is a difficult question; but it is at least true that the elements of the artwork are appreciated for their own sakes: colors, lines, forms, masses, textures, etc. (Some people who say they do not like abstract art, and only enjoy representative art, claim that they cannot appreciate simple elements like lines or shapes for their own sakes. That this is not really true is demonstrated by the fact that they _can_ enjoy purely abstract decoration, on wallpaper, or on textiles, for example, or the

---

5 For a good, though critical, review of the literature on this tradition see George Dickie, "All Aesthetic Attitude Theories Fail: The Myth of the Aesthetic Attitude," in Dickie and Sclafani, op. cit., pp. 800-814.

abstract shape of a new work in architecture.) In being sensitively aware of a work of art these things are experienced as being good in themselves.

A possible objection to the claims that a life could be an artwork and that in such a life moral and aesthetic values would coincide is that what makes art valuable is just that it <u>is</u> separate from life. The idea that art is a respite from the dirt and struggle of daily existence is a fairly common one; art is special and exalted. A view similar to this is held by Clive Bell: "For, to appreciate a work of art we need to bring with us nothing from life, no knowledge of its ideas and affairs, no familiarity with its emotions. Art transports us from the world of man's activity to a world of aesthetic exaltation. For a moment we are shut off from human interests; our own anticipations and memories are arrested; we are lifted above the stream of life."[6]

Bell goes on to argue that it is inferior art and inferior aesthetic appreciation that involves itself in "the emotions of life" or the "ideas of life."[7] When this happens one has ". . . tumbled from the superb peaks of aesthetic exaltation to the snug foothills of warm humanity."[8] Pure appreciation and pure art involve, respectively, the appreciation of and the creation of significant form and, also, the enjoyment of the peculiar aesthetic emotion that these provoke. This view of art (and of appreciation) clearly demarcates it as something necessarily distinct from one's life--the moment the "emotions and ideas of life" enter the artwork (or one's appreciation) one is no longer dealing with pure art (or pure aesthetic appreciation).

A closely related objection, which I would like to discuss together with the one above, is that whereas the moral evaluations we make in our lives require us to take (or refrain from) certain actions, the aesthetic evaluations we make concerning artworks do not impose

---

6   Clive Bell, "Art as Significant Form: The Aesthetic Hypothesis," in Dickie and Sclafani, op. cit., p. 44.

7   Ibid., p. 45 and p. 46.

8   Ibid., p. 46.

similar requirements for action on us. Such a view is defended by Roger Fry, who argues that imaginative life and actual life are quite distinct, and that art is intimately connected to the former and not to the latter.

> Art, then, is an expression and a stimulus of this imaginative life, which is separated from actual life by the absence of responsive action. Now this responsive action implies in actual life moral responsibility. In art we have no such moral responsibility—it presents a life freed from the binding necessities of our actual existence.[9]

Based on a few assumptions from what he calls "elementary psychology" concerning the "nature of instincts,"[10] Fry argued that human beings have ". . . the possibility of a double life; one the actual life, the other the imaginative life."[11] The greater part of our "actual life" is dominated, he asserts, by instinctual reactions and their accompanying emotions. These instinctive activities, Fry claims, constitute the "important part" of our actual lives, and further, that it is toward them that "man bends his whole endeavor."[12] The imaginative life, on the other hand, is quite different and is the basis for art:

> . . . in the imaginative life no such action is necessary, and, therefore, the whole consciousness may be focused upon the perceptive and emotional aspects of the experience. In this way we get, in the imaginative life, a different set of values, and a different kind of perception.[13]

9 Roger Fry, *Vision and Design* (Cleveland: Meridan Books, 1956), "An Essay in Aesthetics," pp. 20-21.

10 Ibid., p. 17

11 Ibid., p. 18.

12 Ibid., p. 18.

13 Ibid., p. 18; see also p. 20.

Fry argues that in aesthetic perception we see events more clearly[14] and feel emotions more purely.[15] This constitutes the difference in perception: ". . . we become true spectators, not selecting what we will see, but seeing everything equally. . . ."[16] The difference in values lies in the claim that in art there is absent responsive action in which we are morally responsible.

Bell's and Fry's positions are similar in that both refuse to consider the *possibility* that events in one's life could be experienced in the way one experiences an artwork (or could be dealt with in the way an artist deals with a medium). Bell never considers the possibility that one could conduct one's life in a way such that it had significant form. (Whether there is such a thing as significant form that all artworks have in common is a separate question.) If someone lived his or her life, *with* all its emotions and ideas, in such a way that *it did* have significant form, then that life itself would provoke, *ex hypothesis*, the aesthetic emotion that Bell claims all true art provokes.

Fry never considers the possibility that one could develop one's awareness in such a way as to be aware of events in one's life (including perceptions, emotions, and responsive actions) with the kind of clarity and purity he reserves for aesthetic perception. But what is to prevent someone from developing this approach to all aspects of his or her life? Could one not perceive and feel the moral necessity for telling the truth in a given situation with clarity and purity? What is to prevent one from perceiving one's morally responsible actions themselves with clarity and purity? Is it not precisely (in part) the artist's and the moralist's capacity to perceive aspects of the world and of experience which most of us miss almost entirely that sets them apart from us? The suggestion I am advancing here is simply that this kind of sensitive awareness could be carried further. If this development of awareness did take place, then one would have the

14   Ibid., p. 18

15   Ibid., p. 19.

16   Ibid., p. 20.

kind of perception of one's life that Fry claims is only possible with respect to art. Fry's reply to this suggestion would be that the domination of instinctual reactions and emotions in our lives makes this suggestion an impossible one. But this "elementary psychology," on which Fry's position depends, needs to be examined somewhat more closely.

Unfortunately, the elementary psychology upon which Fry's entire argument rests is <u>extremely</u> elementary. How it is even possible for us to act in morally responsible ways given that our actions are determined by instinctive reactions, Fry never explains; yet morally responsible action is supposed to distinguish actual life from imaginative life. It is because human intelligence makes it possible to act in ways other than those determined by our instincts (and other conditions) that both morally responsible action and what I shall call "aesthetic action" are possible. Indeed, Fry's own writing is a clear counterexample to his claim that it is toward our instinctive reactions that ". . . man bends his whole conscious endeavor."[17] Surely Fry's essays were not written by a man completely dominated by instinctive reactions, but, rather, by a man who, though possessed of instinctive reactions, was aware of them in such a way that they did not dominate him. This is the true character of human intelligence.

The second half of Fry's argument for the distinctness of art and life is that in aesthetic situations there is an "absence of responsive action,"[18] whereas in life there is both the necessity of responsive action and moral responsibility for one's actions. In many common situations something like this may be true, but there are two ways in which its importance is undermined. To begin with, I have already argued that moral and aesthetic values would coincide in the life of art. Thus there would be little or no difference between one's response in an aesthetic situation in the studio (or gallery) and in a moral sitaution at home. One's response in either case would be based on an appreciation of things for their own sakes (whether colors, for example, or persons).

17  Ibid., p. 18

18  Ibid., p. 20.

Secondly, in arguing that in art there is a complete absence of responsive action it would seem that Fry is thinking exclusively of the role of the witness of an artwork as opposed to the role of the creator of an artwork. Art is something made by the responsive actions of an artist (to his or her medium, among other things). If there were no responsive actions by artists, there would be no artworks. Action is absolutely essential in art. (Further, it could be argued that the role of the witness of an artwork is, in part, constituted by some kind of vicarious experience of the responsive actions of the artist, and thus involves a kind of "secondary" responsive action.) The point is that in aesthetic activity we act on the basis of valuing things for their own sakes, which is the same as the basis of moral activity. If you are a witness of Jones' moral activity, *you* are not obliged to act, though Jones may be. In the same way, if you are the witness of an artist's aesthetic activity (at a dance performance or in a gallery), *you* may not be obliged to act, though you may become aware of the necessity that was (or is) present in the creative activity of the artist.

Another possible objection to the view that a life could be a work of art is that whereas all persons are deserving of equal respect, some art is bad and some is good.[19] That all persons are deserving of equal respect, however, does not imply that they are all morally equal; just as there are good and bad artworks, there are good and bad people. Kant actually argued that capital punishment was the proper way to show respect for a murderer. The moral person does not treat all persons in exactly the same way; rather he or she treats them in appropriate ways based on equal respect for each one. The true aesthete appreciates all artworks for what they are in themselves, and makes critical judgments accordingly.

Both aesthetic and moral judgment share the principle that things can be, and sometimes should be, appreciated for their own sakes. Both morality and art ask us to approach some situations without expectations of good consequences, without expectation of some kind of a return on our investment. There is, often, some

---

19 Sherry Buckberrough suggested this objection to me.

kind of return on this kind of investment; but the kind of satisfaction that can be experienced in this kind of situation is not the sort that can be experienced by seeking consequences. This kind of satisfaction is only experienced when one genuinely approaches a moral or aesthetic situation out of a sense of appreciation for the thing itself.

Since art is concerned with the appreciation of things for their own sakes, it is not surprising that artists sometimes take as the content for their work a social situation in which there is a lack of appreciation. War, violence, racism, and sexism have been treated in works of art in an attempt by artists to point out the absence of appreciation in situations where it ought to exist. There is the danger in this kind of art, however, that the artist will lose sight of his or her task of creating something that can be appreciated for its own sake and, instead, create something that is valued for its consequences only (or primarily). Thus we get art that is merely ideological, and boring. One gets the feeling, in the presence of this sort of work, that one is being preached at--which is hard to appreciate since it does not seem to involve any awareness of the value that things have independently of their consequences. Further, one gets the feeling that the artist, in creating the work, was not appreciating much of anything (at least not for its own sake).

I am not arguing that artists should not be interested in consequences at all. I have only said that when concern for the consequences outweighs the appreciation of things for their own sakes, then we get art that is boring because it does not involve this kind of appreciation. Picasso's Guernica is perhaps a good example of a painting that expresses a sense of outrage with a violent and wicked bombing, but which does not become lost in the sense of condemnation such that the possibility of appreciating things for their own sakes is lost. What comes through from Guernica, at least for this observer, is a sense of an incredibly sensitive awareness of pain, suffering, and outrage; there is almost the sense that even these things can themselves be appreciated for their own sakes. There is sensitive awareness of these things, simply. Somehow this does not seem incompatible with the condemnation implied by the painting.

An apparently powerful objection against my argument in this paper is that it might appear to license aberrant or wicked behavior by allowing the excuse, "It's art." Consider the possibility of a "murder artist" or a "torture artist." The murder artist might argue that he or she uses murder as one aspect of his or her life of art. There is an essay by DeQuincey, "On Murder Considered as One of the Fine Arts," in which some of the fine points that might come up in such a situation are considered in a very humorous way.[20] I have argued that in most cases moral and aesthetic values would coincide. But how could one proceed in a case in which they appeared to conflict?

The murder artist would fail as an artist because it would be impossible for him to genuinely appreciate the life of the person he was murdering. He would thus fail to appreciate the properties of the materials of his art, which, I have argued, is essential for an artist. The "nobility of the material"[21] would prevent the sensitive artist from using human beings (including himself) in certain ways. As an artist, a person is committed to appreciating things for their own sakes. But the murder artist would be caught in an inconsistency in declaring, on the one hand, his appreciation for things in themselves, and, on the other hand, destroying not only the object of appreciation but also the possibility of appreciation in another person. Appreciation would, in effect, be cutting its own throat. Appreciation cannot be true appreciation if it is destroying appreciation.

20  Thomas DeQuincey, <u>The Collected Writings of Thomas Quincey</u>, ed. David Masson (New York: AMS Press, 1968), Vol. XIII, pp. 9-124. DeQuincey also makes the claim that any man who calls himself a philosopher, who has not suffered an attempted assassination, has "nothing in him" (p. 24). It is worth noting that De Quincey produces "evidence" that Spinoza was murdered (pp. 27-28).

21  I have borrowed this phrase from Roger Bacon, the thirteenth century philosopher and scientist, who argued against the use of human beings as guinea pigs in scientific experimentation on the grounds that the "nobility of the material" made the possibility of mistakes unacceptable.

In this paper I have argued that as modern and contemporary artists have tested the limits of what could be used as the medium for a work of art, they have simultaneously explored the boundary between life and art. The suggestion I have made is simply that there remains a final step to be taken, viz., the declaration by some artist that his or her life itself is an artwork, that the complete life is being taken as the medium for a large-scale work of art. The middle section of the paper was an investigation of the relationship of moral and aesthetic values in which I argued that these actually have the same foundation--appreciation of things for their own sakes--and that in the life of art these values would coincide. Finally, I considered the role of moral values in art and the apparent problem of a "murder artist." There could not be a murder *artist* because one cannot genuinely appreciate a person and destroy him or her at the same time.[22]

---

[22] My thinking about aesthetics has been deeply influenced by Chogyam Trungpa, Rinpoche; I wish to express my appreciation. See, for example, Chogyam Trungpa, <u>Visual Dharma Sourcebook II</u> (Boulder: Nalanda Foundation, 1979).

COMMENT: Chris Horton

Professor Bakker's argument is developed in three premises: (1) That it is no longer possible to determine if something is a work of art primarily on the basis of the medium of its expression or construction; "Anything can be used as a medium in creating a work of art." (2) That it is possible for a life to become a work of art--now that all media are tenable. (3) That since art works and persons are best appreciated through a view which holds them both to be "things which are good in themselves," aesthetic criteria and moral criteria may overlap and coincide.

With the first premise, I agree, as it accurately reflects the contemporary situation in art. About Mr. Bakker's second premise I hold some major reservations and his third I see as neither highly probable nor highly desirable.

I am sorry that Mr. Bakker did not address himself more comprehensively to some of the other constructs we employ in describing, analyzing and determining if some object or event is art and not something else, particularly since it is apparent that the criterion of medium is now neutralized. We still consistently apply the concepts of form, content, style, meaning, context, intention, (and I would add imagination and originality to these determinants) in our judgments and evaluations of art.

If I intend my life as a work of art, will that be sufficient to realize such a project and to have it understood by others as such, or will I also have to alter the form, content, meaning, style and context of my life to something other than that which I would have ordinarily pursued? If we believe works of art to be fundamentally imaginative, what would it mean and what would it be like to live my life as a product of my imagination? If we believe that every individual is unique, yet know that the vast amount of art produced in any period is derivative, imitative, repetitive and entirely unoriginal, how do we determine the originality of a life lived as art? How many such lives would we accept as being original works? Indeed, Mr. Bakker is being somewhat of the artist himself, following the conceptualist mode of introducing an idea as the work; moreover, he has precluded the possibility of anyone who chooses to live a life as art of claiming such a work as original--in concept.

Engaging another of the constructs which underpin our definitions of art, how do I go about inserting my life into the art <u>context</u>? Perhaps I could choose to live in a museum. Would I work 9 to 5, be a part-time work of art, so to speak? Or would I have to be on exhibit 24 hours a day for a lifetime? Should I draw the curtains on my aesthetic cell when I sensed that some of my life-functions, behaviors or monologue might offend or provoke some viewers, or "let it all hang out," in the idiom of the popular domain?

Even if Bakker himself decided to execute his idea, its originality is marginal if the only strategy employed is a change of context. Marcel Duchamp initiated this method of art practice when he slipped his urinal into the stream of art discourse under the pseudonym R. Mutt. The '60s and '70s have seen extensive if not exhaustive exploration of re-contexting as an art maneuver which has ranged through live animals, plants, whole ecological systems, life acts, amateur art (as high art), logic problems, dictionary definitions and abstruse private languages. The work of one of the front-line conceptual artists of the 1960s debilitated context as a sole means for deploying art with a work which consisted of the statement, "All of the things about which I am not now thinking."

The recontextualization of life as art would not be a radical challenge to the present status and practice of art, and for such a work to be interesting, original and generative in the discourse of all art, the simple shifts of medium and context would appear to be insufficient. Some alteration in form, content, style and meaning; some change, extension, or redirection in the course of art would have to be initiated by such a work for it to be considered more than an anomoly or curiosity in the art world.

Theory in science holds elegance to be one of its central values; higher mathematics is an almost totally formalized discipline and many other fields of study and endeavor maintain that aesthetic considerations are a relevant component of their activity. As members of American culture we are in danger of becoming totally aestheticized through media and Madison Avenue pandering of the egregious value "life style." Since style is essentially an art term and an art concept one could easily jump to the conclusion that life and art are already conjoined--until one looks at the form, content, meaning and originality of the lives of those fixated by such a goal and sees little but superficiality, artificiality, fad, fashion, conspicuous display and shallow self-centeredness.

Certainly these are not the kind of values we should wish to emerge from a grafting of aesthetics with morality, but even the more respectable principles and qualities of art are not necessarily congruent with or supportive of moral codes and criteria. "Turn the other cheek," and "An eye for an eye," are statements with aesthetic overtones, not the least of which is their mutual reference to symmetry, but their moral import is contradictory.

Although we might hold both persons and art as things which are good in themselves, I don't see how such a belief would help generate the kinds of responses and judgments we make in relation to persons and art. If I had a choice between saving a person in a wheelchair and a Rembrandt painting from a burning museum, the choice would be between aesthetic values and moral values, and to confuse the two brings no benefits to life, art or philosophy.

COMMENT: Sherry Buckberrough

The topics that Dr. Bakker has chosen to discuss are indeed critical issues in assessing the function of art in contemporary Western society and posing hypotheses concerning its function in the future. It is certain that in the history of twentieth century art the dissolution of traditional hierarchies of media has led to a confusion of the realms of art and everyday life. Bronze and marble sculpture, oil painting, and other such art forms sanctioned by age-old academies possessed inherent boundaries as a result of the distinction and permanence of their materiality. Such defining boundaries clarified the spectator's understanding that the work of art was, in fact, a humanly structured realm existing apart from the randomness of the world around it. Those same boundaries of media were also the art work's limitations--the definitions that insisted that art was, however strongly or beautifully accomplished, only an artificial arena. Its artificiality being clearly recognized, the value of art came to rest on the merits of artificial structuring; in other words, on principles of craftsmanship and aesthetics. Art was indeed expected to be an island of clarity removed from both the chaos and the active demands of everyday life.

Artists of this century who have rejected traditional media have in almost all cases done so with the intention of bridging the well established gap between art and life. It has generally been their purpose to allow the aesthetic realm to extend to vaster areas of that everyday life, to bring aesthetic definitions into line with the commonly accepted consciousness of reality (as opposed to artificiality) by using "real" rather than "art" media, and thus to make art both more accessible and more relevant within contemporary culture. However, this attempt at the integration of the realms of art and life has posed as many problems as it has hoped to solve. Dr. Bakker's assertion that an artist could use life itself as art without limitations of material, time or space must be considered against the reality of the problems encountered by artists who have already been involved in a less total manner with these interests.

In Western culture the value of art is determined by the marketplace, despite all attempts to alter the situation. That marketplace includes such institutions as galleries, museums, government and foundation collections and such personalities as critics, curators and collectors who are essential to the spread of information about and the validation of new forms of art. The professional artist works or creates within the confines of this market system.

The folk artist, working outside the marketplace, creates a kind of art that is generally valued within a limited, perhaps even a private realm. Such an artist may very well possess the capacity to "appreciate things for their own sakes" and to create with the sensitivity of that appreciation. The public valuation of the folk artist's work, however, will likely remain minimal. The public's capacity to appreciate may not be as evolved as that of the folk artist. On the other hand, if the work has strong visual impact, usually achieved by aesthetic structuring that distinguishes it from everyday reality, it may be recognized and "appreciated" not only by a broader public but by members of "the profession." Once acclaimed by the profession, the work achieves the visibility necessary to alter public sensitivity and it thus attains higher value in the marketplace.

The professional artist who attempts to fuse art and life by rejecting the limitations of traditional media faces the same problem--that of visual impact--but from a different direction. The work must be recognized as art before it is given credit for being art. If the media used are closely associated with everyday life, the artwork must then distinguish itself through the structuring of the media in time and/or space (i.e., the visual aesthetics) or by a clear statement in verbal or written form of the artist's intentions. The closer the work of art comes to approximating everyday life, the more imperative it is that the artist resort to some clearly artificial device such as carefully planned placement, documentation or explanation, to allow the work to be recognized. The artificial device ensures the separation of the two realms and thereby their recognition. In the attempt to bring art and life closer, the artist often finds that the resulting problem of recognition forces the gap wider.

The proposed conflation of art and life through the breakdown of media hierarchies that has already occurred in contemporary art has engendered corresponding problems of value confusion. Cross-currents arise between aesthetic values, whose evolution toward ever greater theoretical subtlety has resulted from the tradition of "art for art's sake," and moral values, confused by social flux and thrust necessarily into the arena of art by the overlap of life with art. Recent art that incorporates aspects of cruelty, violence, pornography or self-destruction has been seriously challenged by critics and the public as immoral despite its aesthetic justifications. The gap in understanding of values that such art creates renders it generally ineffective. To rectify this confusion there is a need for the formulation of a commonly accepted set of bases for both moral and aesthetic judgements. If it were possible that such a formulation could occur through the "appreciation of things for their own sakes" and the fusion of art and life, serious problems of alienation and philosophical cross-currents would be resolved to the applause of almost all associates of the art profession.

The absolute fusion of art and life is, nonetheless, a practical impossibility. The concept necessitates the dissolution of the profession, a change which is unlikely to evolve from within the art world system. Desirable as such a fusion might be, it would require a thorough revamping of the value system of Western culture and many of its supporting institutions. Furthermore, a life conducted fully as a work of art, incorporating the active responses of astute moral judgement as well as the clarity of aesthetic form (though I find this possibility within the reach of a very rare few, if any, human beings in Western culture), would almost certainly remain unrecognized as art. Such a life would include the subtleties and refinements of wholistic balance, a state frequently sought but seldom noticed in our culture of excitement and extremes. Public sensitivity toward life and art must be redirected before a life of art could be appreciated. Until such a change might occur, the artist must rely on artificial devices to make the art work apparent. A life conducted fully in the realm of artificiality would be a life viewed as insane. The actuality of the total situation of the art marketplace and present Western values would condemn the attempt to public defeat.

PAPER IV

WAR AND MORALITY

Peter K. Breit

To some the fusion of war and morality is oxymoronic. To others it is simply moronic. Militarists either banish morality or, worse, enlist it in their behalf, while the morally attentive condemn war as either anachronistic or so modernly destructive as to defeat any rational ends for which it might be employed. Neither position is, in itself, tenable, and war and morality are not necessarily incompatible.

Two reasons for acknowledging a link between war and morality have been to <u>justify</u> a war and to <u>mitigate</u> its harmful effects. In the first category we find arguments relating to <u>jus ad bellum</u>, the law which is said to govern a polity's entry into war. In the second are the laws which are to control the polity's behavior during war. This is the so-called <u>jus in bello</u>.

Traditionally, <u>jus ad bellum</u> was both generous and restricted. Being unable to obtain punishment of a transgressing neighbor by other means, leaders were to be guided in war by morally right intentions. They were to be morally convinced that responding militarily to injustice produces more good than evil and that justice is served by war. (Cf. Dougherty & Pfaltzgraff, 191.) The difficulties of this approach were recognized during much of history. An effort finally to deal with them was made at the Nuremberg Trials after World War Two. Here one of the three charges brought against the German leaders was that of committing crimes against peace, which fall into the category of <u>jus ad bellum</u>. These crimes involved "planning, preparation, initiation, or waging of a war of aggression [nowhere, however, was there agreement on what aggression meant], or a war in violation of international treaties, agreements or assurances, or participation in a common plan or conspiracy for the accomplishment of any of the foregoing." (Jackson, 100.)

What, however, is one to make of a morally relativistic argument that Hitler was morally convinced of the justice of Germany's cause? I raise the point only to illustrate the difficulties in the just war doctrine, not to plead the morally repugnant case for Hitler. Difficulties are involved in the traditional right to go to war. For one thing, what does one do with such plans or preparations for war as take place purely within the domestic jurisdiction of a polity which intends to go to war? Does <u>jus ad bellum</u> permit potentially aggrieved states to embark on their own preventive or even pre-emptive war? Israel's destruction of Iraq's nuclear reactor in 1981 and Daniel Webster's admission in 1842 seem apt here. Webster acknowledged instances wherein the "necessity of . . . self-defense is, in fact, overwhelming, and leaving no choice of reason, and no moment of deliberation." (Webster, in Moore, 412) Webster points to a critical aspect: choice of means. It is not difficult to understand why. <u>Jus ad bellum</u> will permit pre-emptive or preventive war if no other means are available and if the efforts are made to meet the requirements for proportionality and discrimination. After World War Two, the victorious allies believed they had an answer to the question of war in anticipation of greater tragedy. It is found in the third war crime, the crime against humanity which deals with "murder, extermination, enslavement, deportation, and other inhumane acts committed against any civilian population, before or during the war; or persecutions on political, racial or religious grounds in execution of or in connection with any crime within the jurisdiction of the Tribunal, whether or not in violation of domestic law of the country where perpetrated." (Jackson, 101.) Strictly speaking, <u>jus ad bellum</u> had shifted and became a responsibility for outsiders.

A citizen, Karl Jaspers writes, must "bear the consequences of the deeds of the state whose power governs [him] and under whose order [he lives]." (Jaspers, 31.) Can it reasonably be argued that outsiders, and especially those who might later be called upon either to defend themselves or avenge the violation of <u>jus ad bellum</u>, are "co-responsible for the way [the world] is governed"? (Ibid.) In all likelihood, this position cannot be sustained. It will, however, be vindicated by victory where "success decides." (Ibid.) Here is a clear weakness in the just war doctrine as it relates to permissible conduct prior to war: to punish its transgression requires another to embark on his own just war. That is the logical result of the Nuremberg decisions: the victorious allies ought at least not to have abetted Hitler by their appeasement and should, in fact, have determined the justice and rightness of their cause against Hitler even before 1 September 1939. The question is, of course, when ought they to have made that determination, and how should they have acted on it? To have made it too early would have rendered them guilty of violating jus ad bellum. The essence of appeasement, in fact, was that it was an attempt to leave no peaceful effort untried.

Let us look ahead for a moment. For what kinds of acts might the United States be cited under jus ad bellum? We might be absolved of preparing for a defensive war. But the problem is critical: what distinguishes defensive from offensive war? Does the first unauthorized use of force denote aggression? What constitutes authorized use of force? To what extent does our preparing for defensive war or for peace (si vis pacem para bellum) contribute to another's aggression? Are our armaments intended as "contingency planning and preparation for the lawful use of force?" (Midgley, 262.) That would be sanctioned under the Nuremberg Charter and the United Nations Charter. Second, are the armaments intended for an "unlawful war"? (Ibid.) This would be proscribed. Finally, if the decision-makers have planned and prepared for a surprise attack, that would be prohibited. If, however, Israel and Iraq, for example, have been in a state of sempiternal war, Israel's attack on the nuclear reactor may fall within the guidelines of jus in bello.

Basically, the question of intent governs. Was there an intent to commit acts which violated international law? (Cf. Midgley, 264 et seq.)

Let us move to the second aspect of the just war doctrine, the question of jus in bello. This had been the mainstay of the just war doctrine for it seemed the most amenable to the combatants' individual control. Jus ad bellum had gained the greatest modern momentum in the Kellogg-Briand Pact (1928). It finally seemed possible to determine what constituted aggression—a confidence completely unfounded in reality—while it suddenly became clear that it was quite impossible to "maintain . . . the traditional limitations of the jus in bello in the face of the development of military technology." (Midgley, 67.) This is a vital point, especially in the age of the nuclear missile which is at once able quickly to transcend distance and to bring virtually instantaneous destruction to an opponent. Can war, given its destructiveness, "still be saved?" (Cf, Lindemann, passim.) In other words, has war still a purpose, which is to say one related to meaningful choices and ends?

Serious problems exist when governments intentionally and knowingly issue orders which violate, or command inferiors to violate, the principles subsumed under jus in bello. "If it were not so, then we should be bound to say that the injuries of war are irrelevant to the justice of a war and that the traditional teaching concerning the need for a sufficiently grave cause is merely mistaken." (Midgley, 68.)

In war, as in morality, the critical point may be intelligence or "prospective thinking." This means more than simply anticipating the consequences of one's act, which is largely a strategic or tactical calculation whose object is maximal destruction at minimal cost. Prospective thinking involves considering the question what, given the destructive capacity of modern weapons and the vulnerability of modern targets, can be undertaken without violating the principles encompassed by the jus in bello?

It will be noted that I have included several considerations here. First, there remains still the strategic question (what is the political purpose of the war?). Second, the tactical question endures (what means are employed in order to achieve the strategic objectives?). The first question is generally left to the civilian, that is, political authorities. The questions dealing with tactics are, on the whole, more related to the military instrument whose purpose it is to carry out policy.

The third consideration involves the destructive ability of modern weaponry. Much of the weaponry remains untested, either for its strategic or tactical importance. The danger exists that it will have been its tendency toward success, by which I mean toward unanticipated destructiveness, which remains the critical issue. There is a moral dilemma in permitting arsenals to continue to grow without any proximate confidence that their ability to destroy will not exceed the principle of proportionality. That principle holds that "injury or damage to legally protected interests must not be disproportionate to the legitimate military advantages secured by the weapons." (Department of the

Air Force, 6-2.) In fact, we may be certain that they will exceed what is necessary. They are oversized.

The tendency toward success of any untested weapon may exceed its anticipated ability to achieve its objectives to such an extent that it would, were its tendency toward success demonstrated, be prohibited ipso facto under the principle of proportionality. Should it therefore be prohibited without the demonstration afforded by a test?

The fourth element involves the vulnerability of modern targets. I mean here both military, where the sophistication of weaponry and the expense of training persons to operate them are critical factors, and civilian targets. Vis-a-vis civilian targets, conventional war contained the seeds of unintended or unanticipated destructiveness. One has but to consider the effects of World War Two here. The fire bombing of Dresden in 1945 killed more people (directly and indirectly) than died at Hiroshima and Nagasaki.

Presently total war means the production, concentration, and application of all one's resources, including population, to obtain the complete destruction, viz., annihilation, of an opponent, if necessary. Total war involves survival and the complementary risk thereto. "In total war . . . every effort made implies perforce some possible alternative effort left unmade. There should, in fact, be ultimately no pool of unallotted effort to draw upon." (Garsia, 136.) Here precisely is the question: how, with weapons' unanticipated destructiveness, can a strategist or a moralist approach the problem of total war? I propose that he cannot. In addition, total war, obliterating the characteristics which separate the combatant from the non-combatant, places an enormous burden on the moral aspects of war and of planning for war, be it offensive or defensive.

The political will to wage a total war may be frustrated by the absence of resources. The political will to limit a war may be frustrated by the deployment of new weapons whose effects are not understood.

Some tendencies toward totality result not from accident or design--neither of which may safely be excluded from moral considerations--but from shortages or limitations. Britain, for example, is often accused of waging indiscriminate nighttime bombing in World War Two as though this were a matter of choice. In fact, the destructiveness of British night raids on Germany was the result of an inability to conduct daytime bombing. (Cf., Falls, The Art of War, 155.) What level of moral engagement is possible here? And to what extent was the destruction caused at night an excessive goal, if no other means were available for Britain at least cost to herself to achieve her strategic objective of forcing Germany to adjust her behavior to Britain's wishes? Now, the law of war does address itself to this problem in the discussion of "double effect." Even this point, in which one must evaluate the unintended effect along with the intended, is not unambiguous, and especially not where a polity does not, because there have been no recent tests to evaluate the unanticipated destructiveness, have the information on which neatly to segregate the intended from the unintended effects. Consider, for example, the mistaken view

> that a person of normal psychology would not in practice annihilate a city without having within his direct intention the destruction of the population as well as the purely military objectives which would be destroyed. Indeed . . . it does not appear psychologically possible to avoid including the annihilation of the city within one's direct intention, even if one tried to do so. (Midgely, 385-386, his emphasis.)

Unless we remove the "psychologically possible" from the intellectually probable, the statement is inapt. We cannot gauge the intellectually probable without some externally testable standard. And banning tests, desirable in itself and for reasons of ecological cleanliness, deprives us of such a standard. It is probably correct, however, that "there would be no proportionate justifying reason for permitting the evils arising from the annihilation of a city as an alleged side-effect of an attack upon military objectives." (Ibid., 386.)

Several problems present themselves here. One, how, without tests, can one even estimate the extent of destructiveness which would justify fears of "evil" and "annihilation"? Two, what is one to do with such weapons as the neutron bomb which seem to treat each tank as a city in which the crew and not the vehicle is to be destroyed? It is well and good to argue that the crew are military persons and as such are vulnerable. Given the destructive capacity of weapons and vulnerability of targets, it is difficult not to extrapolate from the tank crew which merely guides and activates the tank to the civilians who stoke and feed the industries which produce the tank and the shells, and muster the crew.

What, furthermore, is to be done with the moral dilemma of benign as contrasted with malign double effects? The civilians who "also serve" also benefit, although not necessarily in ways obviously related to war. Admittedly, defense and national security are benefits, but they are the benefits derived from war and for which the war is fought. How shall we deal with the double effect of improved medical care available to the civilians after the war? How shall we deal with miraculous fibers, with wonder drugs, with chips and computers, all of which are side benefits of the military effort?

An additional political and moral factor involves the relationship between the domestic political order and the conduct of war. It was once possible sincerely to argue that only certain regimes linked constant expansion and destruction in order to maintain the momentum necessary for their own survival. Now one can no longer be quite so sure that this is an aberrant condition restricted to a particular political system. We have all become too much contaminated by the fusion of destruction and momentum. The problem has its economic aspects as well, as the contradiction between nuclear non-proliferation and sales of weapons and reactors to willing purchasers indicates.

It is indeed a moral dilemma that war is increasingly marked by the absence of restraint, which derives in part from assessments of particular situations, but also in part from the inability to make other assessments. As an example of an inducement to the diminution of restraint one might consider the reasons for the decision to drop the atomic bomb in 1945, reasons which in retrospect seem dubious to some. To those making decisions in 1945 two closely intertwined considerations dominated: (1) assurance of a speedy end to the war with (2) the fewest possible American casualties. As an example of another inducement one might ask why Churchill, with the evidence before him that Germany's bombing of London had failed to defeat the British, should have assumed that strategic bombing of Germany would defeat her.

The seeming contradiction between war and morality emerged in pre-nuclear or conventional war. It reflected an awareness that while conducted by polities, war is fought by individuals who, being able to destroy each other and able to observe this destruction, can also reason their way out of the fatal entrapment war causes. Until World War One, war involved honor and elan as well as romance. That war, however, buried, somewhere in the sludge and among the crowbait, the detritus of war's romance. And with it went much of the honor and spirit. Seen as a human activity, war was also seen as something which would be mitigated. Efforts were made to curb its worst effects, not so much by eliminating war as by restricting its exercise (jus ad bellum) and magnitude (jus in bello).

An added difficulty for one who wishes to make moral evaluations lies in the fact that weapons in conventional war tended to be single-purpose. This was helpful to avoid escalation by accident as an opponent knew with what the weapons were armed. Today, because aircrafts' "load can be conventional or nuclear . . . their usefulness is . . . seriously restricted in a conventional conflict." (Strachey, 121-122.) Wherein would the moral evaluation lie? In stating that it is wrong to have multi-purpose aircraft? What, then, about the helicopter which can strafe an enemy target but also pluck one's own troops to safety?

One must, among countless others, consider the moral tension between "retrospective planning" which may inflict less harm on an opponent than on oneself, and attributing to modern weapons all sorts of miraculous "quick fixes." We find this often combined in a single approach: planning for the last war while claiming that particular weapons have revolutionized war itself. One manifestation of this approach has been to integrate new weapons as though they were on the same revoluationary level as their predecessors, without considering the effect of the last weapons' tendency to do the same thing. The result is that the development of new weapons outpaces the intelligent ability to reconcile them with strategic, political objectives, not to mention moral responsibilities. Weapons begin to dictate tactics and tactics, strategy. Finally, strategy begins to enjoin morality. And this is a fundamentally immoral condition.

The appearance of new weapons has regularly produced both exaggerated hopes and overstated fears. Weapons believed to be unusually destructive are often proposed as the reasons for the permanence of peace. The appearance of new weapons has also engendered a superficially reasonable response: let us find new ways of protecting ourselves against the weapons. Unfortunately, protection, especially in the age of deterrence, is exactly what one does not want, if by protection one understands security, which is to say freedom from care. The frequently proposed shelter program is an example: people who are "secure" in their shelters ordinarily do not have the larger public interest, namely the desire to avoid their polity's devastation, in their hearts or minds. Such interest derives from the community of being insecure along with one's fellows. Shelters, and it is irrelevant here whether they do in fact protect, encourage not only freedom from care but carelessness. Not only do they therefore threaten to undermine efforts to stabilize the environment within which both contradictory polities and weapons exist, but they raise the question of the post-attack environment. What are the moral implications of encouraging people to believe in a life after Armageddon? One can also not forget to ask what is to be done with those who either cannot afford or cannot reach shelters, or even with those who simply will not build them.

Recalling our central thesis that in war and morality prospective thinking, defined as anticipating consequences and realizing that the combination of destructive capacity and vulnerability of targets severely limits what may be done without violating the principles in <u>jus in bello</u>, we must add further elements. Industrial and technical developments during conventional war served to cheapen human life, not primarily by often rendering manpower unnecessary, but by consigning it to slave-labor and to initial and final lines of defense. It is difficult to argue that this does not violate the precepts of jus in bello.

This point is even more clearly made when one considers that war, the ultima ratio regnum, mobilizes the traditional "elements" or "ingredients" of national power:  geography, population, economic strength, condition of resources, administration, education, and morality, and attempts to guide them toward a successful conclusion.  If that is not possible, it ought to direct them toward a defeat with the least possible destruction consonant with the stronger side's objectives.

Propaganda, often used to weaken an enemy's population, reflects the user's view of war.  Why has propaganda become so important?  It is, after all, generally not directed against the enthusiastic supporters of the adversary's position.  War involves an ever-increasing dependence on urban areas.  Cities, the hallmarks of western civilization, have become its greatest weakness.  Strategically the emphasis has shifted from the battlefield, with its one-man, one-bullet calculus, to the modern city.  Here, in the intellectual, financial, moral, and industrial fulcrum of life--and hence, war--almost everything on which the fighter depends is produced or prepared for combat. First, because of an inability to hit them directly rather than for humanitarian considerations, cities became targets for propaganda.  Civilians, viewed as a war's weakest elements, were in effect used against their leaders.

Thereafter, cities became logical targets for internal physical and economic attack.  Sabotage's destructive effects and the certainty that it can be instigated from without, even short of war, as in Germany's undermining of Austrian or Czech resistance, is the twentieth century's emendation to an older doctrine.  Internal pressure is then combined with external obliteration of frontiers and violations of territoriality.  Here the airplane is vital.  It is viewed as a means of destruction and of producing terror, often linked with the navy to create a blockade to induce economic collapse.  But, as World War Two demonstrated, air power served also as a means of injuring and killing refugees who were attacked as means of "chok[ing] the hostile army's means of communication." (Falls, The Nature of Modern Warfare, 6.) Questions of proportionality and discrimination surely emerge here. These are now further in doubt as a result of "stealth" technology wherein approaching aircraft are rendered invisible to radar.

It has been another feature of war that each side misgauged the resilience of populations, ascribing heroic resistance to its own and cowardly flight to its adversary's. Or, at other times the enemy's citizenry was believed to be stronger and more resistant. Enemies are seldom simply "human." Not one of the problems I have raised can be regarded as adequately considered by our strategic planners so long as they do not know what is, reasonably, to be modern weapons' tendency toward success. This becomes more critical when a further factor is added.

All wars end. This is not to say that they end neatly or with peace treaties; it is just to say that the fighting at some point ceases. There will perhaps be the question of surrender. It is first a moral and political--not military--question whether the surrender is to be in the form of a bilateral contract in which victor and defeated are bound by a series of obligations and rights, or in the form of an unconditional surrender which practically gives the victor carte blanche in his treatment of the defeated. (Oppenheim, 553. See also Kecskemti, passim.) In either case, it would seem, Victor Hugo's observation holds: "To the victor belongs the responsibility for peace."

Other moral dilemmas present themselves. There is, for instance, the 1944 attempt to kill Hitler. The conspirators attempted to kill him, not because they were agreed on what should follow him, but as an act of tyrannicide. On the surface this would be justifiable. But what are we to do with the danger, clearly to be anticipated, that success in assassinating him would spark a new stab-in-the-back legend? Is this not somewhat related to the central theme here that it is not enough to anticipate the consequences of one's act. One must worry about violating the principles underlying the law of war. Assuredly one such principle is not to allow those responsible for the war to escape answerability. For Hitler, as for any one guilty of crimes against the traditional laws of war (jus ad bellum and jus in bello), to evade answerability is to allow him to escape the promise he is assumed to have made to those who supported him: to enter a war for just reasons and to fight it with just means. To have killed Hitler would have shifted the onus for the now clearly lost war to his killers, where it plainly did not belong, from its chief architect (by his own claims and admissions). This is another example of the double or unintended effect. Those who were really morally concerned about the war would have to wait another ten months. To have left even the slightest hope that Germany could win the war, that Hitler could escape the condemnation of his own people, would have been catastrophic.

It is indeed an aspect of morality and war that the victors often appear to have been as brutalized in the process of victory as the defeated were in their efforts. By 1945 conventional war had passed beyond relying on an opponent's exhaustion and shortages of resources to bring him to surrender. War had become annihilative. It had become limitless. Thirty years earlier Freud had said something rather striking about our topic and about civilization. The Great War, he said

> shattered our pride in the achievements of our civilization . . . and our hopes for a final triumph over the differences between nations and races . . . . [It] revealed our instincts in all their nakedness and let loose the evil spirits within us which we thought we had tamed for ever by centuries of continuous education by the noblest minds . . . . [It] showed us how ephemeral was much that we regarded as immutable. (Freud, 81-82.)

He suggested that the result of this being "bereft" was to intensify man's nationalism.

World War One began the modern process of diminishing man's confidence in a global civilization and morality. It would appear that World War Two completed the job. So, it is not surprising that the architect of that war, Hitler, should have written that his

> pedagogy is hard. The weak must be chiseled away . . . . I want a violent, arrogant, unafraid cruel youth . . . .

Nothing weak or tender must be left in them. Their eyes must bespeak once again the free, magnificent beast of prey . . . . I want youth that are athletic. Thus will I erase a thousand years of human domestication. (Vogt, 163.)

Here we have not only the tension between one who cared for civilization and one who declared war on it. We have an example of a man, who while fortunately probably rare in his ability to conceive of total destruction, i.e., tendency toward success, was also in a position to shape and guide events in directions others thought incredible. He was able to imagine a world so dazzled and shocked by the sheer arrogance of his claims that nothing he could do would seem to violate the principles of either <u>jus ad bellum</u> or <u>jus in bello</u>. In fact, for reasons beyond the scope of this assessment, neither principle of the just war tradition ever acted as a restraint on Hitler.

We have also an excellent example of a crime against peace. And we have a clear example of the theme of these remarks: morality and war do not concentrate or begin on the battlefield. Precursors of and antecedents for that mortal and moral engagement we call combat are found, if they are found at all, in the civilian sector. These, too, involve prospective thinking where we are made aware not only of the destructive capacity of modern weaponry, but--more tellingly--of all that makes life modern, meaningful, livable, and vulnerable.

## Notes

1. Dougherty, James F. & Pfaltzgraff, Robert L. Contending Theories of International Relations: A Comprehensive Survey. 2nd ed. New York: Harper & Row, Publishers, 1981.

2. Falls, Cyril. The Nature of Modern Warfare. New York: Oxford University Press, 1941.

3. Falls, Cyril. The Art of War. New York: Oxford University Press, 1961.

4. Freud, S. "On Transcience." Sigmund Freud's Collected Papers. James Strachey, ed. Vol. V. New York: Basic Books Publishers, 1959.

5. Garsia, Clive. Planning the War. Harmondsworth, U.K.: Penguin, 1941.

6. Von Glahn, Gerhard. Law Among Nations. 2nd ed. New York: MacMillan Publishing Co., Inc., 1976.

7. Jackson, Robert H. The Case Against the Nazi War Criminals. New York: Alfred A. Knopf, 1946.

8. Jaspers, Karl. The Question of German Guilt. Trans. E.B. Ashton. New York: Capricorn Books, 1947.

9. Kecskemeti, Paul. Strategic Surrender. New York: Atheneum, 1964.

10. Lindeman, Helmut, ed. Ist der Kreig Noch Zu Retten? Frankfurt: Fischer Bucherei KG, 1965.

11. Midgley, E.B.F. The Natural Law Tradition and the Theory of International Relations. New York: Barnes & Noble Books, 1975.

12. Oppenheim, L. International Law: A Treatise. H. Lauterpacht, ed. New York: David McKay, Inc., 1955.

13. Moore, John B. International Law Digest. Washington, D.C.: Government Printing Office, 1906. Vol. II.

14. Strachey, John, in Heilbrunn, Otto. Conventional War in the Nuclear Age. New York: Frederick A. Praeger, 1965.

15. U.S. Department of the Air Force. *International Law: The Conduct of Armed Conflicts and Air Operation*. Washington, D.C., 1976.

16. Vogt, Hannah. *The Burden of Guilt*. Trans. Herbert Strauss. New York: Oxford University Press, 1964.

COMMENT: Julian W. Streitfeld

Wars are horrible and destructive, and yet those who fight in them, and even those who make wars, are for the most part, not sadists who enjoy inflicting pain on others, not individuals intent upon hurting people and destroying their possessions, but principally average, middle class individuals who would not think of hurting their neighbors, or other human beings whom they see as being like themselves. There have been some notable exceptions, including some sadists who take pleasure in inflicting pain upon and hurting others. They may seek out wars as situations in which they can find their gratification. But they are a small minority among the vast numbers who engage in wars. Most wars are probably made for "good" and "moral" reasons by people who believe they are doing what is "morally" right. This matter of wars being fought by average middle class individuals who get no joy out of human pain and destruction has been illustrated in a number of pieces of literature and art forms. The relatively recent television program "The Holocaust" portrayed one of the most ardent Nazis as a lawyer who came from a middle class family and was a good husband, father, and neighbor. Human beings like this perceive in others a similar humanity, and identify with them, thus finding it difficult to hurt, much less kill or plan wars for their destruction. Another illustration is a television movie which I recall having seen several years ago. It showed a man who didn't give a second thought to dropping bombs which killed hundreds, perhaps thousands, of people, but who had significant problems and misgivings when faced with the situation of having to kill a person face to face by cutting his throat and watching the look of horror on the victim's face while doing so.

A third illustration of this point is the "War Prayer" written by Mark Twain. It shows the bloody destruction to the enemy, and the misery brought to their loved ones as the consequence of victory by their own soldiers.

People, when thinking about the glory of war and the conquests of their own soldiers, may well ignore the consequent bloody results of such conquests. Again, the point is that people find it difficult to even contemplate the horrors inflicted on other human beings.

Finally, a recent program on Public Television, "Kitty Returns to Auschwitz", again demonstrates the difficulties of even the victims of this horror in seeking revenge. Kitty was a former inmate of Auschwitz. In a sequence filmed for the television program, she returned there with her son. After reviewing with him all the suffering she had experienced and the torture and death which she had witnessed, she said that at the end of the war some of the surviving inmates marched out with a passion to kill any German they would come upon. They went into a building where they saw some frightened individuals huddled in a corner and they couldn't carry out the violence they had planned. She said, "We couldn't be like them", referring to the camp guards, the SS, and all their oppressors.

I believe, however, that what was involved, as they saw the individuals huddled in fear, was an identification with them as human beings, and they couldn't do things which would hurt them as they had been hurt.

Thus, in order to make war, to get ordinary common people to engage in its violence, several things must be done. For one thing, the participants must be removed from the victims of the war. It is much easier to drop bombs from several thousand feet above, or to push buttons from hundreds or thousands of miles away, or to sit back and make decisions and plans when the humanity of the enemy is out of sight and awareness than to be where one sees the face of the victims in pain and death. By removing the active participants from the victims, they can be kept from having to face the direct, immediate consequences of their actions upon human beings.

Secondly, to make war it is necessary to dehumanize the enemy. For this purpose the machinery of propaganda is highly utilized. The enemy is portrayed as some variety of "untermenschen"; he is vermin, infecting the body politic as the Nazis portrayed the Jews, Gypsies, Slavs, and other victims. During the Second World War, American propaganda identified the Japanese as the "little yellow bellies" or "the yellow menace" in books, newsreels, movies, cartoons, comic strips and various other sources of public information. Himmler, the Chief of the Nazi SS in World War II, was reported to have told his SS executioners how wonderful they were to be able to eliminate the equivalent of interior beings while they themselves remained civilized and fine human beings. These descriptions and portrayals tend to remove the humanity from the victims, making it easier to aggress against and destroy them.

A third thing that contributes to the ability of ordinarily non-violent, non-destructive individuals to make war is the induction of fear. If individuals are to kill the enemy it is very helpful for them to believe that they must do so for fear of otherwise being killed themselves, by the enemy. Two things come to mind: one from literature, and the other, a report of an actual experience.

In the book <u>All Quiet on the Western Front</u>, the German hero is shown killing the French soldier, initially out of fear that he himself would be killed. When his fear abates he sees the dying and then dead French soldier as another human being and feels intense remorse for his action.

The other incident I heard from a soldier who was in the Korean war. He, the American, had fallen when being overrun by the Chinese Army, and saw standing above him a Chinese soldier with a gun aimed at him. The Chinese soldier hesitated a moment before pulling the trigger. In that moment of hesitation, this individual killed the Chinese soldier. Why did the Chinese soldier hesitate? How did this American feel about killing the Chinese soldier? Why would either kill the other?

Another change that has to take place to make the peaceful middle class individual a killer in war is the pressure of authority, telling him what to do. The fear of punishment by authority for not complying is only part of the explanation, but the fear does tend to inhibit resistance to the voice of authority. A number of studies by Stanley Milgram, a social psychologist at Yale University, illustrates how easy it is for an authority figure to get ordinary, kind, middle class individuals to act in a way they believe inflicts pain, even the apparent possibility of death upon innocent victims. It appears that those individuals, like most of our fellow citizens, tended to relinquish responsibility for their actions to the authority figure. When the authority has power over one, the tendency to obey is even greater. Involved in this type of behavior seem to be long established habits of obedience to authority, reluctance to disobey, and fears of disobedience, and of authority.

A fifth condition which influences a change in the average citizen is peer pressure. The attitude that because "everyone is doing it", so one also should do it; it would be shameful to "chicken out". It is easier to comply with such pressure than to resist. The threat for any resistance is that of being belittled and ostracized. The refusal to go to war when there is a draft takes tremendous courage because it frequently is in opposition to peer pressure as well as authority. Once in the service, the peer pressure to comply, which comes from one's squadron, company, battalion, etc., becomes just about insurmountable.

Among the consequences of these various efforts and pressures upon the individuals is that they are changed and engage in war and its related destructive activities against their more ingrained inclinations. They, themselves, consequently often become dehumanized, and with that, often experience psychological distress upon removal from the pressures and propaganda when they see more clearly the behavior in which they engaged. To protect themselves from such distress, individuals tend to deny responsibility for their actions. They may claim "it is not my fault, it is that of others". The individuals in Germany and Japan who had participated in the war atrocities blamed the leaders for their actions. They hid behind the claim that they were "just following orders". The individuals denied responsibility for their own behavior. The leaders, on the other hand, denied responsibility claiming that they did what they did, not for themselves, but for the benefit of their country and the people.

What are some of the motives which motivate these "good" and "moral" people to make war? What are the benefits for those making and planning wars? For one thing there are the benefits of prestige and honor. These may involve achieving ideological goals. For Hitler and the Germans it was the establishment of the Thousand Year Reich which, with its "racially purified" superior people, would dominate the inferior ones, at least in all of Europe. For the Soviet Communists it is the establishment of the greatest good for the greatest number, as they see the "good" to be.

There is current fame and future renown for the heroes of wars, be they leaders or the actors on the field.

Another motivation is the achievement of benefits by such groups as munition makers, and for the economy as a whole. Bertrand Russell expressed a wish to the effect that: God protect us from the moralists who have done more destruction and more killing than all of the declared criminals. It appears that the war leaders all proclaim that morality is on their side. Are they the moralists of whom Bertrand Russell spoke?

What can be done to overcome these various pressures to engage in war? It would be interesting to consider going back to primitive times when knives, stones, and clubs were the highest technological, or development level, for war. In Michener's historical novel, Centennial, he spoke of one of the largest wars between Indian tribes or groups of tribes in which no more than a few hundred people were killed. But who wants to give up the comforts and benefits which accompany the advances in technological warfare? Its impossibility would probably bring a sigh of relief to most people.

Another approach might be to train individuals for responsibility earlier in life. In Nuremburg, the principle of individual responsibility was declared and emphasized. The World War II Allies declared that those who were found to have engaged in war crimes could not hide behind "obedience to authority" as a means of escaping responsibility for their actions. Individuals should learn to attend and respond to their consciences, and to take responsibility for their actions. Individual responsibility should come to take precedence over national or group responsibility. If, for example, individual conscience and responsibility were to be in conflict with a national war movement, individuals should learn that it is better to comply with their consciences, and, where conscience directs, participate in protest movements and, if necessary, evade conscription and/or war service, being willing, of course, to take the consequences of their behavior, rather than to comply and ultimately become dehumanized where compliance violates their consciences.

Another thing that might be done to help individuals follow judgment and conscience rather than to follow the leader blindly, is to rehumanize the enemy. This happened in the Viet Namese war. When soldiers went into villages and saw the children they had killed, and when television brought the enemy victims into the living room at dinner time, people could see that the "horrible" enemy were not monsters, but other human beings, like themselves.

Another approach to overcome social pressures would be to downplay "blind obedience to authority." We may have to pay a penalty for this, as parents with children entering adolescence, but it may be a relatively small price to pay for the resultant individual responsibility.

As Americans, and a free people, it is important that we protect the Bill of Rights, as is being done by the American Civil Liberties Union. For individuals to be able to act upon conscience and judgment, factual knowledge must be available to them. For this we need a free press and freedom of speech to combat the propaganda, and the right to petition and to protest. In this way individuals may find common grounds and the support of others in their resistance to the pressures of a powerful, organized government.

In conjunction with the above suggestions, we might also consider moving from national to individual morality with respect to participation in acts of war. One more word about morality. Morality is both cognitive and emotional, both of which individuals learn. Cognitively, it is a value such as right and wrong. Emotionally, it is a conditioned reaction which leads to approach or avoidance.

Finally, it is suggested that some of the re-enforcements for war be removed, such as the profits and other economic benefits and gains. Let us question, and not blindly accept, some of the ideologies that promote war.

Dr. Breit asked why, when the German bombing of Britain was not effective in bringing the British to their knees, did the Allies, particularly the British, attempt to achieve that precise goal by the same methods. (As Dr. Breit pointed out, German war production even increased during the most intense strategic bombing). We turn to an appeal to reason and intelligence for answers. It appears, however, as though reason and intelligence may very well be less determinants of behavior than the tools and mechanisms to serve the person in achieving gratification of emotionally determined wishes and goals. Reason and intelligence may determine more the means than the goals.

Still, we can and we must try to move in the direction wherein human intelligence rather than human emotions dominate in the determination of our behavior. Only thus can we most reasonably use knowledge, and judgment, as well as our consciences, in making our important decisions.

COMMENT: James Etzwiler

Professor Breit has raised a cluster of fascinating, knotty questions about the morality of modern warfare. And he does so by referring to a host of particular episodes from recent history which point up the difficulty of determining when an act of war may be judged ethical. We in philosophy tend to be much more chaste in our course with facts which probably explains why our solutions seem so much more clear and neat.

He is surely correct in claiming that it is at best paradoxical to speak about the morality of war, but the paradox is certainly not one that only the 20th century is confronted with. Was it much less peculiar for medieval theorists to defend the morality of splitting one's enemy's head with a great axe or of bashing in his sides with an iron truncheon? Nevertheless this near absurdity appears particularly evident in our time when the instruments of war have become so devastating of population and geography.

I want to make but two brief observations on the many points which Professor Breit has raised: one is an observation of fact, the other one of principle. First I would like to inject a timid note of optimism here. It is certainly true that in one important sense modern warfare has manifested a lack of restraint. Weapons have gotten increasingly destructive and less discriminating about whom they destroy. But from another point of view we often forget that we've made it from 1945 to the present without a global confrontation of nuclear powers. Parts of the world have been convulsed in savage wars but we have in fact refrained from engaging in a war where nuclear weapons might be employed. In neither Korea nor Vietnam were we seriously tempted to use our nuclear capabilities. And we can surmise that the Russians will show at least that much restraint in Afghanistan. Of course this record could be blemished quickly, but we have survived at least three and a half decades without using or being attacked by nuclear weaponry. In this sense we have in fact learned to restrain our might, if not out of moral scruple than at least out of fear of a disastrous reprisal.

Now to the moral point. I am not wholly certain just where Professor Breit comes down on the issue of whether a nuclear war can be moral. He does contend that total war cannot be morally justified (page 12). Yet he thinks that one can speak of war and morality together. And he gives evidence that most recent wars have been fought with at best a tainted morality. Accordingly one could easily grow cynical about ever addressing the topic of war from a moral perspective. It is tempting just to declare that all modern (and certainly nuclear) war is immoral.

And yet if we succumb to this temptation, we abandon any attempt to restrict the conditions under which modern warfare might be fought. After all, if all modern (and especially nuclear) war is immoral, then a nuclear war of aggression or for aggrandizement is no worse than one fought in defense of one's homeland or of some moral principle. Consequently, we must try to distinguish the circumstances in which nuclear war may be licit and the manner in which nuclear weapons may be used. If we do not try to put some restrictions on this sort of warfare, we may have to face nuclear war with no restraints at all. The same warning applies to germ warfare and to chemical warfare. It is always tempting to the moral person or to the ethician or to the saint simply to exclaim that war--modern large scale wars especially--cannot be justified. But to do so is simply to withdraw from the debate and to allow the politicians and the military strategists to decide the parameters of modern warfare.

I conclude with a final reason for wanting to continue the difficult and at times bizarre task of discussing the morality of war. This effort to make ourselves face the problem of whether nuclear war can be ethically fought will serve to goad us to develop weapons with more refined ranges which can be used with greater precision and control. It may also serve to keep our politicians and military planners conscious of the moral dimension of their grisly plottings. The principles of the just war are, of course, ideal, immensely difficult to apply and rarely if ever perfectly exemplified in practise, but we need them as goals and as an expression of our aspiration finally to live with our fellows in peace.

FUNDERBURG LIBRARY
MANCHESTER COLLEGE

WITHDRAWN
from
Funderburg Library